OH, SOCRATES!

TRACKING THE LIFE AND DEATH OF SOCRATES

JILL DUDLEY

Published by
Orpington Publishers

Origination by
Creeds Design & Print Ltd.,
Bridport, Dorset
01308 423411

Cover design by
Creeds Design & Print Ltd.

© Jill Dudley 2023

ISBN: 978-0-9955781-3-5

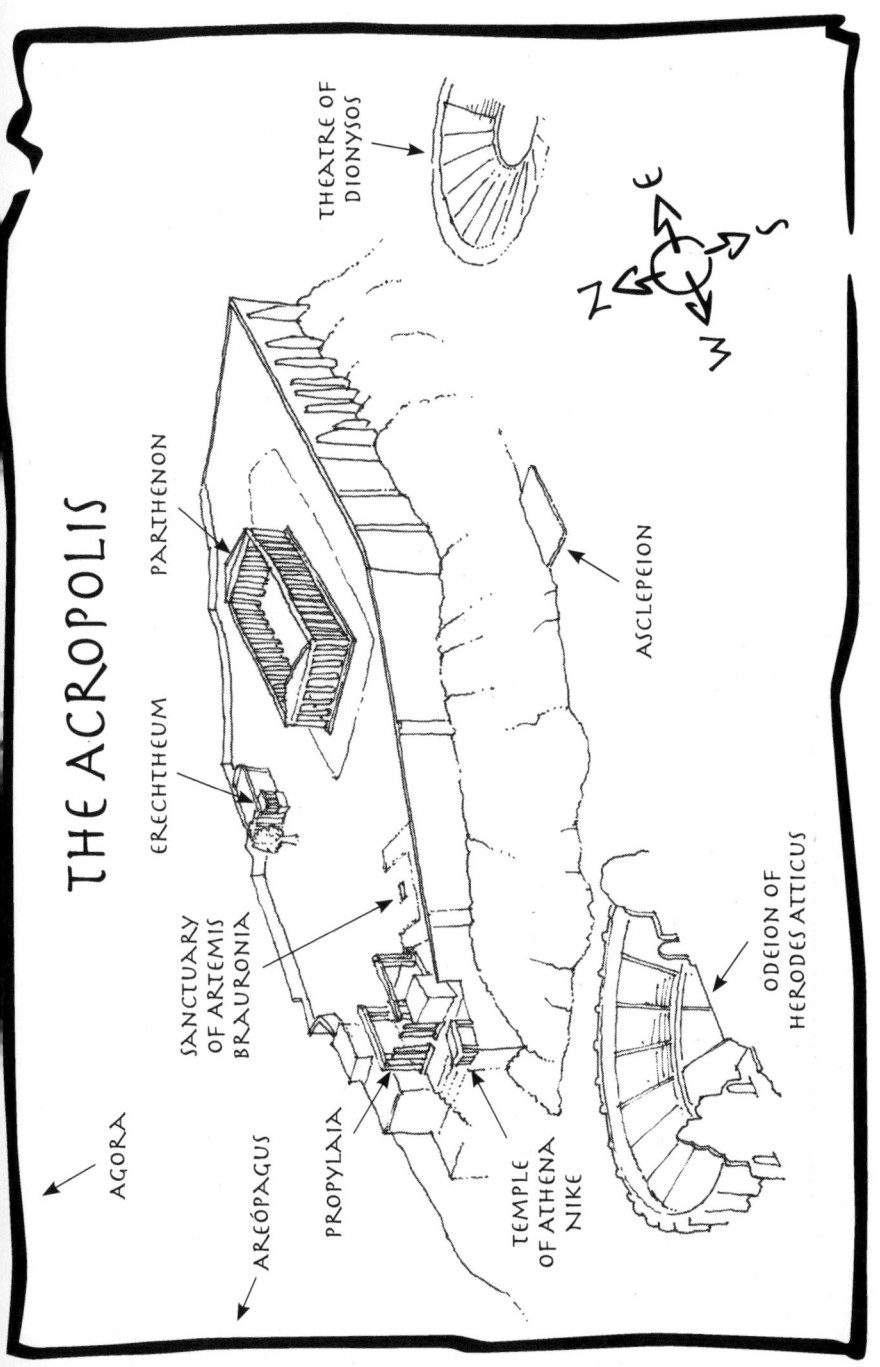

THE AGORA

SACRED WAY TO ELEUSIS

PAINTED STOA

BASILEIOS (ROYAL STOA)

OATH STONE

ALTAR OF 12 GODS

STOA OF ZEUS

PANATHENAIC WAY TO ACROPOLIS

HEPHAISTEION

KOLONES AGORAIOS HILL

BOULEUTERION

METROON

ALTAR OF ZEUS AGORAIOS

MONUMENT TO THE EPONYMOUS HEROES

RACE TRACK

THOLOS

WATER CLOCK

TO PIRAEUS

SOUTH STOA

PRISON

N / W / E / S

CONTENTS

Page

PROLOGUE

CHAPTER 1   1
Athens at the Time of Socrates
Athena's Panathenaia Festival

CHAPTER 2   19
Demeter's Eleusian Mysteries
The Drama Festivals of Dionysos

CHAPTER 3   37
Plato's *Symposium*
Aphrodite, Goddess of Love

CHAPTER 4   51
Plato's *Apology*
The Law Court and Socrates' Trial

CHAPTER 5   61
Apollo and his Twin Sister Artemis

CHAPTER 6   79
Socrates' Last Few Days of Life
Plato's *Crito*

CHAPTER 7 — 89
Poseidon, God of the Sea

CHAPTER 8 — 103
Socrates' Death
Plato's *Phaedo*

CHAPTER 9 — 121
Asclepius, God of Medicine and Healing

EPILOGUE — 129

APPENDIX — 133
The Battle of the Cowshed — 133
God and the Brain — 149
Olympian God in Mourning — 159

BIBLIOGRAPHY — 169

GLOSSARY — 173

INDEX — 193

PROLOGUE

This book is a non-academic book for non-academics. It is written for those who have heard the name of Socrates but know little more about him except, perhaps, that he was condemned to death and died from drinking hemlock.

I have for many years been interested in Socrates and the gods of his day. In this book I write about his life and times in Athens, describe the reasons why at the age of seventy he stood trial, was found guilty of impiety and corrupting the minds of the young, and condemned to death. I also draw on my own past travels to Greece in search of the old Olympian deities, as well as some curious personal experiences.

Over the years of exploring and reading about Greece, I've been astonished by the numerous imaginative stories woven around the Olympian gods, many of them so strange that it is almost incomprehensible that they were imagined at all. Yet the gods were taken seriously and the temples are a proof of the honour in which they were held.

Oh, Socrates! is not about Plato's dialogues, in many of which Socrates can be extraordinarily tiresome and hard going. Yes, I touch on a few of Plato's dialogues to illustrate some aspect of his life or to draw attention to an interesting idea, but that is all.

My aim (as with all my books) is to inform but also to amuse and entertain and in this, I hope, I have succeeded.

CHAPTER 1

ATHENS AT THE TIME OF SOCRATES
ATHENA'S PANATHENAIA FESTIVAL

Many years ago, after a long and tiring journey by bus from the Peloponnese to Athens, Harry and I took a taxi to our hotel and were immediately caught up in a traffic-jam.

Our middle-aged, unshaven taxi-driver was in a filthy mood, and my polite opening gambits at Greek conversation to justify the expense, were either ignored or responded to with gruff, dismissive grunts. He sighed heavily, banged impatiently with his forearms on the steering wheel, and became even more irate as daredevils whizzed past us in the bus-lane. His bad temper was contagious and I quietly seethed with rage, while Harry, who normally has the patience of a saint, grumbled irritably about the damned extravagance of taxis stuck in traffic-jams, and how we could have got there faster had we gone on foot.

After half an hour of stop go, stop go, we lurched left at some traffic-lights (his bad mood was taken out on his taxi too) when, quite unexpectedly, we saw the Parthenon on the Acropolis radiant in the evening light; its off-white marble columns and pediment were a translucent rosy hue reflecting the setting sun. Its impact was immediate, and with it all fury evaporated, even our driver calmed down. The beauty and splendour of something great lies within and breathes from it – it has soul.

Today the ancient temples in Greece, whose few remaining columns draw the eye, are a reminder of the old Olympian gods of Socrates' day. They are awe-inspiring in their balance and simplicity standing as they do in harmony with the landscape, often on sites already considered sacred.

A young Athenian woman once said to me that the Greeks had always been aware of the spiritual, and that nothing had really changed from pagan times. When I asked her what she meant exactly, she said that the people today go to church, not because they believe the Christian dogma, but to celebrate the eternal Mystery. The eternal Mystery? I liked the honesty in that, as it seemed to me that was what all religions were about.

Socrates was born in 469 B.C. in Alopeke, a village which once nestled in the foothills of the Hymettos mountains outside the city walls of Athens. His father was a stone-mason, and his mother a mid-wife. Socrates was known to have married Xanthippe, a woman who bore him three sons, and had a reputation for having a shrewish tongue. When asked how he coped with such a wife, he had apparently replied good-naturedly that anyone wanting to become a good horseman had to be able to manage a high-spirited horse.

Socrates' childhood coincided with the years when the great statesman named Pericles, thanks to his extraordinary genius, his vision and political astuteness, enriched Athens. He did this by imposing tribute money on her colonies and allies in the Delian League, formed for defence purposes against the ever present Persian threat. With the money he was able to fulfil his vision for Athens, and undertake a massive building project on the Acropolis with the Parthenon as its crowning glory. Remarkably, there were many living at that time who had outstanding talent and skill enabling Pericles, not only to fulfil his vision, but to surpass it.

But where do such inspiration and vision come from? Dare I (the God-doubter) suggest that such things are implanted by the gods? All right, by some powerful spirit then — a divine, invisible energy perhaps, which we call God? And, once implanted in the human mind, it is left to the individual to give it birth? How else can we explain it?

There was one thing that Socrates never doubted and accepted as infallibly divine, and that was his 'inner voice' as he called it. It was his 'inner voice', he claimed, that guided him throughout his life; his 'inner voice' which, when he was seventy, brought him to the ordeal of standing trial for impiety and corrupting the minds of the young. It was his 'inner voice' which prompted him to accept calmly the verdict of his fellow citizens and his eventual execution.

How can I, the God-doubter, admit that I once had an 'inner voice' that spoke to me? Unlike that of Socrates, though, mine spoke once only. *Do what you have to do, and then you'll be free*, the quiet, clear voice had said. At the time Harry had just bought a dairy farm and, because there was no money to employ anyone, I became his farm labourer. It was the daily chores — fetching in the cows, preparing and washing down the dairy, feeding the calves etc. etc. etc. — which I found repetitive and irksome. One evening I was feeling particularly frustrated and rebellious, and just wanted to bang my head against a concrete block or metal pipe. Suddenly, and quite unexpectedly, the small voice spoke very clearly: *Do what you have to do, and then you'll be free.*

Do what you have to do?

I took it to mean that I needed to get things better organized.

And then you'll be free. Yes, that surely was what it meant: I'd be free to write, to read, to learn Greek. But what then made me want to learn Greek suddenly? Was it an 'inner voice' guiding me in a direction I had never formerly thought of going? Have I been responding to an 'inner voice' all these years without knowing it? Well, not a 'voice' but an 'urge' giving me the enthusiasm and staying power to write and study?

From then on I organized a daily morning routine for both Harry and myself. I rose much earlier every day to bring in the cows for milking, and did what farm work was obligatory, after which I found I had two hours free to do what I wanted every morning.

Those two hours became sacred to me, and the family knew I was on no account to be disturbed unless there was a crisis. It was that 'inner voice' that put me on the right path to sanity. And Harry recognized my need and gave me all the encouragement I could hope for.

It was during these sacred hours that I wrote short nonsense pieces such as my satire on farm life, entitled the *Battle of the Cowshed*,* a spoof showing how words ruled the world and manipulated humans to do what they dictated. To my surprise it was broadcast on Radio 4, as was another crazy story *God and the Brain** in which God regrets giving Man a brain.

---

* For those who would like to read either, see the Appendix.

★

Socrates was thirty-one by the time the Parthenon was completed, standing in all its majesty and glory. Not only was there the Parthenon on the Acropolis, there were other spectacular buildings too, and the young Socrates may well have seen the marble for all this construction work quarried from Mt. Pentelicon, and trundled down the mountainside on rollers; have watched the stone-masons and sculptors (possibly his own stone-mason father amongst them) at work, chipping and grinding and polishing; and seen the columns, frieze and pediments lifted into position on the Parthenon.

Socrates' curiosity was boundless. It was the Agora (market place) that was to be his favourite stamping ground. In the words of Xenophon, a former student and friend of Socrates, whose jottings were collected and published in his 'Memoirs': ...*early in the morning he* (Socrates) *used to make his way to the covered walks and the recreation grounds, and when the Agora became busy he was there in full view... He talked most of the time and anyone who liked could listen...* (Xen. Memoirs 1.1.8)

Socrates was no beauty. He was solidly built, pot-bellied, and had protruding eyes and a snub nose. He must have had great self-belief and a magnetism which drew people to him.

But the Agora was not just a place where people worked, marketed their wares and mingled together, it was the civic centre of Athens. At the north end was the great Altar of the Twelve Gods (from which all distances from Athens were calculated). Close to that was the Royal Stoa, also known as the Stoa Basileios. It was presided over by the King Archon, a democratically elected figure. It was the King Archon who was responsible for all trials of a religious nature, and it was in the Stoa Basileios court that Socrates was eventually to stand trial charged with impiety.

Socrates himself admitted that he found some of the stories about the gods difficult to accept, though Xenophon wrote that nobody ever saw Socrates do, or hear him say anything that was heretical or irreverent.

Considering some of the strange legends regarding the gods, it would be very odd if Socrates did not question the truth of some of them. I too find many stories in the Bible (said to be the divine word of God) difficult to believe. As a child, where I was fed Bible stories about God working miracles, Socrates and his young friends were told stories from Homer's *Iliad* and his *Odyssey* in which the gods and goddesses played a major role supporting the Greeks or Trojans: how they guided an arrow to its intended target; or how they instilled greater energy and speed into the limbs of a favoured hero, had lifted him away or cast a mist around him to save him. Brought up and educated on these epic poems, Socrates was imbued from birth with the interaction between gods and men, as I was with the Almighty.

"You don't honestly think everything in the Bible is Gospel truth?" I once asked Harry – Harry is my dear husband and once long-time travelling companion, till he threw in the towel and implored me to find younger, more energetic companions to travel with. "The wise men, or Magi, following a star, for example?" I said. "I mean, have you ever followed a star? It's a nonsense story."

Harry at the time was totally absorbed in the falling stock market. I didn't know why he got so anxious when it fell. It only fell, as far as I could make out, in order to go up again, and how could it go up if it hadn't fallen? The law of opposites, as Socrates would have said.

There in the Agora Socrates liked to discuss the finer points of language and the purpose of life. He mixed with rich and poor alike, the low-born and the high-born; the artisans and shop-keepers, and the politicians. He questioned anybody who cared to join him in arguing the truth of everything: what was meant exactly when one spoke of Courage, Virtue, Knowledge and suchlilke.

If Socrates' wife Xanthippe was shrewish, it just may be that Socrates was a very trying husband. Tradition has it that, though trained as a stone-mason, there is no evidence he ever worked as one. He practised frugality, possessed only one cloak and went about barefoot. Philosophy and talking in the Agora didn't bring in an income because he refused to accept payment – unlike other philosophers who demanded money first before speaking. Had Harry spent his time in the market talking about Love, Courage, Virtue and suchlike, I might well have become shrewish like Xanthippe. Even more so if he was known to deliberately seek out young men – allegedly to examine their intellectual excellence, but was that all he was seeking out? Plato's dialogue *Symposium* has Socrates taking part in an evening's discussion on Love, revealing that homosexuality was very much an accepted part of life in those days.

Socrates wrote nothing down himself; speak yes, but write, no. In Plato's dialogue *Phaedrus*, he argues that written words are much like paintings of people. You can not ask them questions because, as he puts it, they preserve a solemn silence. I would argue, though, that written words may well be silent and unalterable on the page, but oh, how readers can become fired up by them! How people can shout, disagree, and stamp the ground over them! –

books on theology being the prime example.

In many of Plato's dialogues the word 'God' with a capital 'G', as opposed to 'gods' is, frankly, surprising; but apparently in those days they sometimes used the singular with a capital 'G' to cover the Olympian deities collectively, or else to refer to Zeus only – Zeus, supreme god of the twelve Olympian gods, lord of the heavens.

So what was it about the Parthenon which began as a mere vision in the mind of Pericles? It was built in honour of the virgin goddess Athena – the word Parthenon comes from 'parthenos' (Greek for 'virgin'). Its sculpted marbles depicted stories which had been passed down from deepest antiquity – stories which Socrates would have learned in infancy. For instance, the marbles on its east pediment portrayed the birth of Athena from the head of her father Zeus. Apparently, after seducing the Titaness Metis, Zeus learned that on this occasion Metis would give birth to a daughter but, if he impregnated her again, she would bear a son who would overthrow his supremacy. Because of this he swallowed her whole so she could never conceive by him again. In due course, so the story goes, Zeus developed a migraine, so painful was it that he bellowed in agony. It is said that Hephaestus (god of fire and metal-work) split open the divine head with an axe, and out sprang the goddess Athena fully armed and ready for battle.

The great god Zeus' own birth had been as strange as Athena's and, as I wrote in the Prologue, one wonders how the human mind can conjure up such stories. Zeus' father had been Kronos (Greek for Time); Kronos was the son of Ouranos (Heavens) and Gaia (Mother Earth).

Kronos married his sister Rhea but, when he learned from an oracle that he was to be overthrown by one of his offspring, Kronos swallowed each child as soon as it was born (another swallowing to get rid of a threat). Rather naturally his wife became enraged by this paranoid behaviour in her spouse so, with the birth of Zeus, she hid him in a cave on Crete and gave her husband a stone wrapped in swaddling-clothes to swallow instead.

Harry and I once visited the cave – the Diktaon cave high up in the Dikte mountains in central Crete. Let's face it, humans like to clothe their legends with hard factual locations to give them a semblance of truth.

The following is what I wrote in my notebook shortly after the visit:

'The mouth of the cave yawned at us as we approached. At its entrance steep wooden steps with a handrail descended into its depths. Exhausted visitors were arriving up them, and either smiled triumphantly at us, or were so wearied by their exertions they could only double up to get their breath back.

'Awesome was the best word to describe its interior; a Gothic cathedral in which you could almost hear the shudder and crescendo of organ music. Lit by discreet lighting, the cave walls were sculpted by nature in perpendicular patterns, and were of an oily dark hue in sombre shades of jade and deep amber. Its lofty height and width were astonishing. Spiritually uplifting? Oh, yes!

'We descended to the rock-floor of the cave where there was a small lake; its waters were as clear as glass and revealed the numerous coins which people had thrown in, using it as a wishing-well for their own unspoken hopes and fears.

'We could only stand and stare around in silence. A

cathedral demands silence and hushed whispers. One last look at the majesty of this lofty cavern; another glance at the sheet of perpendicular folds said to be the shawl of the infant Zeus, and we bagan the long, steep climb up the numerous steps towards the light again – from the dark and the ancient past, we came up to the sunlight and the present day.'

Since time immemorial Zeus was believed to rule the world from the summit of Mt. Olympus, home to the Olympian gods. Near the Mytikas peak an immense scallop-shaped rock, known as the Throne of Zeus, was where he was said to survey the world of men.

Any fool can climb the mountain, I'd been told, before we ourselves attempted it. It is easy to be an intrepid mountaineer whilst seated in an armchair, but quite a different matter when toiling up through forests of bottle-green conifers alongside precipitous ravines, and knowing there are many more hours of uphill slog before reaching the refuge-hut. It was there we planned to stay the night so that the following day we could tackle the higher peaks to see the Throne of Zeus.

But oh, how that night in the refuge-hut I tossed and turned with dread at the thought of going higher the next morning; of crossing a narrow ridge where, I'd been warned, faint-hearted climbers often suffered from vertigo. It was there also that hikers were sometimes caught out by clouds suddenly boiling up from below and enveloping them. 'Easy to walk over the edge,' someone had quipped.

How relieved I was when, at the first light of dawn, Harry called out mournfully from his bunk, that his back had seized up in the night and he certainly couldn't walk higher, he only hoped he could get lower.

Our slow descent of Olympus gave me all the time I

needed to feel the gods around me.

Here I will quote from Hesiod, an eighth century B.C. poet whose work Socrates would have been familiar with. His words paint a vivid scene of Mt. Olympus where the Battle of the Gods and Giants took place – a battle also portrayed on the Parthenon marbles, and not to be confused with the Battle of the Gods and Titans which had occurred a generation earlier. The Giants were an aggressive race whom the gods had finally overthrown in order to rule the world. They were reputedly monstrous beings like humans but with serpents' tails attached to their feet or legs.

Hesiod describes how the sky quaked and Olympus was shaken to its foundations by the onrush of the immortals throwing themselves on their adversaries: ... *The great earth rumbled, and broad heaven groaned, shaken; and tall Olympus was disturbed down to its roots, when the immortals charged... Zeus no longer checked his rage, for now his heart was filled with fury, and he showed the full range of his strength. He came from heaven and...from his mighty hand the bolts kept flying, bringing thunder-claps and lightning-flashes, while the holy flame rolled thickly all around... (Hesiod. Theogony)*

Some years later, when I was staying in a hotel at Litochoro, the picturesque town at the foot of Mt. Olympus, chosen for its views to the mountain, I sat out on the balcony late one evening and watched a thunderstorm over the mountain peaks. I was very conscious that Zeus was popularly known as the 'gatherer of clouds' or 'thrower of thunder-bolts'.

The black clouds swept across the sky in my direction. The rumble of thunder drew nearer, and fork lightning streaked down from the sky. Soon it was overhead. Just beyond the hotel was a church with a gabled roof on the top of which was a floodlit cross silently proclaiming Christianity to the world. Suddenly there was a flash of lightning and an immediate crash of thunder, and all the lights of the town went out. The Christian cross and the church were blacked out. I saw it as a battle between the Olympian gods and Christianity – a sudden uprising and a moment of triumph when the Christian cross was wiped out by Zeus' lightning flash. In no time at all, however, the electricity returned and Christianity triumphed once again.

The occasion inspired me to write what I called Lord *Zeus in Mourning*,* a piece about how the great god Zeus had been ousted (without realizing it until it was too late) by the Son of the Jewish God.

But I have deviated somewhat, and must return to Athens at the time of Socrates.

The King Archon at the Stoa Basileios in the Agora, as well as being responsible for trials of a religious nature, was also in charge of the major festivals in Athens, the most important being the Panathenaia in honour of the goddess Athena.

The Panathenaia was an annual event held around July. Every fourth year it was celebrated with greater pomp, and was known as the Great Panathenaia. It was the Great Panathenaia procession that was portrayed in marble on the Parthenon frieze.

The frieze ran around the top of the Parthenon's colonnade (one hundred and sixty metres of it), depicting horses rearing and neighing, young men on horseback, marshals, chariots, musicians, youths carrying water-jugs,

---

* For those interested, see my *Olympian God in Mourning* in the Appendix.

CHAPTER ONE 13

magistrates, bellowing bullocks being led for sacrifice, young girls carrying ritual implements together with libation bowls and so on.

The brilliance of this flow of movement set in marble, captures the moment of the procession as it must have appeared to the eyes of Socrates standing in the crowds lining the Panathenaic Way.

The Great Panathenaia celebrations lasted a week, during which time many events took place: there were boat races held in Piraeus harbour, competitions for recitals of Homer, musical contests, athletics and equestrian events; and just east of the Altar of the Twelve Gods in the Agora was a race-track for horse and chariot races.

It wasn't till the Parthenon was fully constructed in 438 B.C. that Phidias' famous gold and ivory cult statue of Athena, nearly twelve metres in height, was dedicated to her at the Great Panathenaia festival of that year. There the goddess of the city stood, tall and resplendent, a gold crown on her head. She wore a long, draped robe, and over that her aegis, a waist-length garment portraying the head of Medusa – a head that had writhing snakes for hair, a hideous face and glaring eyes which reputedly turned all who saw it to stone, hence it being a protective garment. Her shield, on which one hand rested, had on it a battle scene, while on the upturned palm of the other hand was a winged Nike (the personification of victory).

And that was what it was all about: Victory! Athenian victory over her enemies – Persian defeat.

All ninety-two metopes, great sculpted slabs, positioned just below the roof of the Parthenon, depicted past victorious battles, each side of the Parthenon showing a different conflict. At the east end was the all important Battle of the Gods and Giants which had brought about the rule of the Olympian gods; on the west showed a battle between the Greeks and men in oriental dress, thought to be the Persians; along the long north side were scenes from the Trojan War; and on the south side was the battle between the Lapiths and the Centaurs (strange creatures, half-man, half-horse).

Since they came into the world as a result of Zeus for once showing concern for Hera, his long-suffering wife to whom he was constantly unfaithful, I will relate their story now – it is one of mythology's wilder tales, the truth of which Socrates might well have questioned.

One day, apparently, Hera had cause to complain to her dear husband about a mortal named Ixion who was lusting after her. In response Zeus laid a trap for him by fashioning a cloud in Hera's image. Concealing himself, he watched as the duped Ixion immediately raped it. Caught in the act, Zeus had Ixion fastened for eternity to a revolving wheel. From this rape, however, Ixion fathered a monstrous son named Centaurus who, in his turn, impregnated the wild mares of Mt. Pelion from which centaurs were born with the body and legs of a horse, and the arms and head of a man.

The centaurs were unruly, lascivious creatures who took after their grandfather Ixion – there was only one who was not, and he was exceptionally good and wise; this was Cheiron who became so well respected that he was appointed guardian and tutor to many of the early heroes such as Jason (of the Golden Fleece) and Achilles (of Achilles' heel and Trojan War fame). There are several caves in the Mt. Pelion area which claim to be Cheiron's cave, one of which a young man named Dimitri and his friend Spiros took Harry and me to see. To quote again from my notebook at the time:

'They led us down a track which began to plummet steeply into a deep forested ravine. Having no head for heights I grabbed Dimitri's arm and used him as an anchor as we descended – down and down through the autumnal gold- and bronze-leafed mountain trees. After about four hundred metres we manoeuvred round to the right where there was a widish ledge. Spiros and Harry were already there beside large grey boulders. Their cave turned out to be a huge gaping hole in the ground over which was laid a cattle-grid type covering to prevent anyone from falling into what looked like a bottomless cavity.

'Dimitri and Spiros stood either side of it smiling expectantly, waiting for a show of enthusiasm from me. I dutifully said it was amazing, but I also looked at the plummeting forest. For Cheiron to have a cavity in the ground here? It would be a major feat to climb out of it, even if you were half-horse, or even all horse. But for the young heroes who'd been under his care with only two legs and two arms? How would they have managed?' I certainly didn't think that cave gave legend factual evidence in any way at all.

Apart from Cheiron, the other centaurs were quarrelsome in the extreme and were often at war with the Lapiths, a neighbouring nation in Thessaly. A great skirmish occurred between them at a wedding to which the centaurs had been invited: they drank too much wine, became thoroughly obnoxious and, quite disgracefully, attempted to abduct the bride. The result was a fierce battle, a scene that is frequently to be seen on temple friezes as it is symbolic of good winning over evil, right triumphing over wrong. And Socrates would have approved as he never ceased to search for the good in everyone, encouraging all and sundry to lead virtuous lives, something which was picked up centuries later in the teachings of Christ.

★

Back again to Athens!

I will end this chapter with another occasion when the Parthenon stamped an indelible impression on my mind. Harry and I were on a rooftop restaurant which had a view to the Parthenon. It was a warm, balmy evening and we were relaxing after dinner with glasses of wine. Our waiter stood by our table, and so began a strange conversation. He was holding a small round tray against his stomach which he turned and turned while shifting his weight from one foot to the other. He was slim, middle-aged with large sombre eyes and amusing eyebrows which slanted upwards giving him a slightly anxious expression. We'd just learned from him he was unmarried.

"You're probably happy that way," I suggested.

"No, I'm not," he said.

"Oh, dear, I'm sorry. What's the trouble?"

"I'm never happy," he replied.

"Never happy? You must have a reason," I said.

"No. It's how I am," he said. His face had a comical dead-pan look like Charlie Chaplin.

"What can we do to help you?" I asked.

"There's nothing you can do," he said, moving his weight from one foot to the other and turning his small tray.

"Don't you have any family? Brothers or sisters? Parents?"

"They can do nothing,"

"Do they live nearby?"

"No, my home is Olympia."

"Oh," I said brightly, "that's nice, Olympia."

"But I never go home."

"No girlfriend?" I enquired.

"I have nobody," he said.

"I'm sure you'll find somebody soon," I said soothingly. He had quite a pleasing face with his verging-on-the-comical expression. "You'll suddenly meet somebody and everything will change. Next time I come to Athens I'll find you happy."

"I don't think so. Maybe I don't want to be happy," he said with a slight note of defiance.

"I can't believe that," I said.

"Maybe I enjoy being sad."

"Well, in that case – " And I sank back in my wicker chair despairingly. "If you enjoy being sad, maybe you're happy after all!"

"Not everyone wants to be happy," he said with finality and, with a little bow, he went back to his duties.

"Funny fellow," Harry said.

How Socrates would have loved him, and would have wanted to define the word Happiness!

By this time night had fallen. Harry raised his glass, and with a nod, indicated I should look behind me. I turned in my chair, and there was the Parthenon, floodlit and resplendent on the Acropolis with a full moon hanging in the sky above it. The waiter's gloom and sadness were instantly forgotten. Although stripped of many of its marbles, the Parthenon stood majestically as Pericles had planned it should, and as Socrates had seen it: a unique symbol of the eternal Mystery – the Mystery that the young Greek woman had once spoken of.

CHAPTER 2

DEMETER'S ELEUSIAN MYSTERIES
THE DRAMA FESTIVALS OF DIONYSOS

Another deity of extreme importance at the time of Socrates was Demeter, goddess of corn and agriculture. How can a city survive if its citizens have no food? It was Demeter who established what became known as her Greater and Lesser Mysteries. They celebrated the annual death and resurrection of Demeter's daughter Persephone (otherwise known as Kore, meaning 'daughter'). It was as true to pagan thinking then as Easter is to the Christian world today.

Demeter's Greater Mysteries, set off from the Altar of the Twelve Gods in the Agora. Socrates, no doubt, would have been amongst the crowds watching it depart.

It was about fourteen miles to Demeter's sacred sanctuary at Eleusis, located to the west of Athens. At the time of Socrates it was surrounded by prairie-like cornfields known as the Rharian plain with a backcloth of distant mountains to the north, and the Saronic gulf and offshore island of Salamis to the south.

But, oh, how ugly and depressing are the surroundings today! To get there now from Athens, the road follows what was Demeter's ancient Sacred Way but which today is the main motorway to the Peloponnese. In this modern age you no longer see a peaceful rural scene, but pass factory buildings, depots and warehouses, cement and petrochemical plants, tall factory chimneys and gas-works. And when the bus follows the coastal road, you look out at giant cranes, wharves and old, abandoned rusty container ships. The Eleusian sanctuary is now a little-visited oasis at the heart of a clutter of off-white, flat-roofed houses on rising ground, from which you can only glimpse the sea over roof-tops.

The story of how Demeter came to enlighten the world with her Greater Mysteries is one Socrates would have been told at his mother's knee. The story is as follows: One day Hades, god of the underworld, seeing Demeter's daughter Persephone picking wild flowers in a meadow, seized and dragged her screaming to his kingdom in the underworld where he made her his bride.

Anguished by the disappearance of her child, Demeter searched the world for her. In due course she came to Eleusis, disguised as an old crone, where she sat beside the Kallichoron well and wept. She was discovered there by the daughters of the then king who, seeing the woman in distress, invited her back to the palace. There she was welcomed by the queen who appointed her nurse to her baby son.

Demeter fed the child on ambrosia, the food of the gods, and by night attempted to immortalize him by holding him over the flames in the hearth. One night the queen caught her doing this and was horrified, whereupon Demeter threw off her disguise and showed herself to be the great goddess she was. She then informed the king of her secret rites which were to be revealed only to whoever was initiated into her Mysteries. From that time on these Eleusian Mysteries were celebrated annually in September, and a temple in honour of Demeter was built on a terrace above the Kallichoron well.

The gods had a problem though. While Demeter continued to mourn the loss of her daughter, she ignored her agricultural duties so that plants and all growing things began to wither and die. Not only were mortals starving, but the gods suffered because they received no sacrifice since there was nothing to sacrifice. What was the point in being gods if there was no one to sacrifice to them! Something had to be done, and urgently.

Eventually the Sun whispered to Demeter that her daughter had been given in marriage to Hades by Zeus. Zeus was obliged to order him to release her to the upper world to put an end to all the withering and dying. And so it was agreed that Persephone could stay above ground with her mother for eight months of the year during the spring and summer, but over the four winter months she was to return to her husband in his subterranean kingdom.

Today, at the ancient sanctuary site at Eleusis, there is still the Kallichoron well to be seen where Demeter mourned the loss of her daughter. Turn your back on the well and you will see on a higher level the ruins of Demeter's temple to the right, and to the left all that remains of a temple of Hades behind which is the dark mouth of a cave (today no entry allowed). It was there that Persephone was dragged screaming down to the kingdom of Hades – or to make it a happier story, from where Persephone returned every year to her mother after her winter months in the underworld.

More important for its message of hope and joy was Demeter's temple, her Telesterion as it was called, and her Greater Mysteries which brought the expectation of some sort of resurrection after death. It was something, the truth of which Socrates looked forward to discovering for himself as he awaited execution in his final hours.

In those distant days death was treated with the greatest respect by those still living, as it is today. Every care was taken to see that the deceased went on his last journey appropriately according to tradition. The generally accepted idea being that the dead went down to Hades where Charon, the ferryman, rowed the corpse across the river Styx to the entrance to Hades. The deceased would have a coin placed under his tongue as payment to Charon. At the entrance to Hades was Cerberus, a monstrous beast of a watchdog with three heads and a snake's tail; he would fawn on new arrivals, but attack those who tried to escape. I imagined the imagery was taken no more seriously than the one of St. Peter standing at the pearly gates of heaven with a bunch of keys to allow the newly deceased to heaven, or to cast him (or her) down to hell; or the picture of heavenly angels playing harps, or little black devils stoking the fires of hell. The equivalent of hell in pagan times was Tartarus, and those who'd lived unblemished lives were sent to Elysium (also known as the Islands of the Blessed).

It is not known whether Socrates was an initiate in the Eleusian Mysteries, but certainly Alcibiades (more of him later) was. So also were many of Socrates' contemporaries such as the dramatists Aeschylus, Sophocles and Aristophanes and, no doubt, Pericles, since the Telesterion (Demeter's temple at Eleusis) was part of his building programme and was completed under him.

Those initiated in Demeter's Mysteries undoubtedly believed in the sacredness of their celebrations. At some stage after dark at her Telesterion, there had been a sacred pageant which told the story of the abduction of Persephone, and the misery as Demeter searched the world for her, before the final joy of their reunion. During the pageant the night had been pierced by bright flashing illuminations with shadowed tableaux, whilst the priest intoned the story of Persephone's descent to the dark and fearful halls of Hades. When the return of Persephone was proclaimed, an enormous gong was sounded to simulate thunder, and fire erupted through a hole in the temple roof.

Finally, the most sacred and secret things (known as the *hiera*) were revealed by the priest. What these secret things were has never been revealed. The second century Christian theologian, Clement of Alexandria, did his best to denigrate the Eleusinian Mysteries and, with the *hiera* in mind, declared that he blushed even to think of them; but, as he was never initiated, and it had remained a profound secret on penalty of death if they were ever revealed, how could he have known? To infer they were the lewdest and most obscene objects imaginable was, no doubt, a Christian attempt to defile pagan customs.

At some stage towards the end of the pageant, when the priest was portraying the terrors of Persephone's descent into the underworld, an ear of corn was held up in a moment of profound silence, symbolizing eternal life and resurrection.

An ear of corn! The Christians, no doubt, laughed; it was nothing to the Resurrection of the Lord Jesus Christ himself! All baptized Christians could expect resurrection.

My first ever trip to Athens, was timed to coincide with the Greek Orthodox Easter, and I was astonished at the number of people crowded into the churches for the Holy Week services. At the midnight Resurrection service, I was accompanied by a friendly Greek woman, Kuria

Alezaki, whom I'd met at our hotel. When she learned that I'd come specifically for the Orthodox Easter, and that I had persistent doubts regarding Christianity, she took me in hand. "You ask too many questions," she'd scolded, taking my arm as we'd made our way to a small Byzantine church close to the Acropolis. I had been there for the Good Friday morning service and, to my amazement, had seen a middle-aged woman suddenly prostrate herself at the foot of the crucified Christ fixed to a large wooden cross. Nobody had paid her the slightest attention, and I supposed she must have broken some commandment. I couldn't imagine ever prostrating myself in such a public manner, however guilty I felt. In fact, the more guilty I was, the less likely would I want to draw attention to myself in that manner. Harry would have been the first to haul me to my feet had he seen me make such a public display of myself.

"If you do as I do, this will be good for you," Kuria Alezaki said as we entered the church for the Resurrection service, and immediately began setting an example of Orthodox piety by making numerous signs of the cross as she kissed various icons. "Please – excuse us, my friend from England wishes to see the Resurrection," she kept murmuring as she gradually drew me forward through the crush of people standing till we were near the *iconostasis* (the sanctuary screen covered with icons) which stood before the altar.

The glistening mosaics in this small Byzantine church reflected the light from the many candles; the glinting brass chandeliers and ancient icons, the gleaming white marble pulpit and the carved and gilded bishop's throne, all exuded a feeling of sanctity.

The entrance to the sanctuary was a sliding central

door depicting Christ holding a chalice. At one point the door was tested on its runners and Christ slid from view as the door was drawn aside; a moment later he slid back into view, closing off the sanctuary. The sliding door was (like my faith) there one moment, gone the next.

Just before midnight, the antiphonal chanting between the priest and *psaltoi* (male chanters) built up to a climax. The lights in the church were switched off leaving all in darkness except for the glimmer of four icon lamps hanging before the *iconostasis*. There was an air of increasing expectancy, just as there would have been at Demeter's Greater Mysteries. Kuria Alezaki handed me a white candle with a gesture indicating I should follow her lead.

Midnight!

The central door of the *iconostasis* slid back and, against the black interior of the unlighted sanctuary, the bearded priest in rich vestments stood before the altar holding a single lighted candle. He advanced and pronounced the words *'Christos anestei!'* ('Christ is risen!'), and everyone responded with *'Aleithos anestei!'* ('He is risen indeed!').

At the same moment the church bells pealed deafeningly in sharp bursts, and fire-crackers were let off outside. I was thrust forward by Kuria Alezaki to light my candle from the priest's new 'Light of the world'. There was a certain honour in receiving it directly from the priest, and then lighting the candles of others behind.

When we emerged, having pushed our way out through the crush, I was astonished to find there were as many people crowded into the courtyard and in the surrounding streets as in the church. They had all been listening to the service relayed to them from loud-speakers. Believers, agnostics, the indifferent, all carried white, lighted candles;

all had come for the eternal Mystery that young woman had once told me about.

★

Another festival of great importance in Athens was one of drama in honour of Dionysos, god of wine and drama. The Great Dionysia festival, often referred to as the City Dionysia, was an annual five-day celebration. It was held at the end of March or beginning of April, when the weather could be relied upon for visitors to sail in from the Greek islands and colonies. It was a highly regarded and popular event for all and sundry, and Socrates was one of its keenest enthusiasts.

There was another rather less important drama festival also, known as the Lenaia held in late January. It was at the Lenaia that new, unknown playwrights first tried out their work.

The City Dionysia festival began with a colourful procession which set off from the Agora. Following the Panathenaic Way, it wound around the base of the Acropolis to its south side where, in the south-east corner, was the sanctuary and theatre of Dionysos Eleuthereus ('Eleuthereus' means 'Freedom'). In the procession a wooden image of the god was borne on a chariot followed by ecstatic women devotees known as Maenads, along with men dressed as Satyrs who danced and sang to the accompaniment of pipes. The Maenads (or Bacchantes as they were also called), were mostly women whose ecstatic trances gave them such superhuman power that they were able to run into the nearby forested mountains, and tear apart wild animals and devour the flesh. Such behaviour, of course, prompted the wry comment from Harry that it was just as well Christianity had come along to put an end to all that stupid nonsense. "Ecstatic women! Ridiculous!"

Socrates was thirteen when the tragic playwright Aeschylus died, so he would have been eleven when the great man produced his prize-winning trilogy, the *Oresteia*. The young Socrates may well have been taken by his parents to see it.

Because certain features of the *Oresteia* reappear in later chapters in this book, I will recount it briefly here. The tragedy centres around the return home of King Agamemnon from the Trojan War. Having survived ten arduous years of raging battles, he arrives back at his palace at Mycenae where he is welcomed by his outwardly loving but treacherous wife Clytemnestra. During his absence she has been having an adulterous affair with her husband's cousin Aegisthus whom Agamemnon had appointed regent whilst he was away. Clytemnestra does not want her husband back, so that same night she brutally murders him in his bath.

Their young son, Orestes, is sent into exile but, when he reaches manhood, he is told by the Delphic oracle that it is his positive duty to avenge his father's murder. He obeys the oracle and kills his mother but this immediately awakens ancient goddesses known as the Furies; these women never fail to rise up from their subterranean slumbers to harass and torment anyone guilty of family murder. They are described by Aeschylus as being ... *dark of hue and altogether hideous, breathing out their snorting breath in gusts not to be borne, distilling from their eyelids drops of hate.*

Orestes is driven demented by their constant torment, and he returns in desperation to Delphi to ask the oracle what he should do to rid himself of them. The oracle advises him to go to Athens to seek the judgement of the goddess Athena. This he does, and his trial is held on the Areópagus, a low, rocky elevation some hundred metres to the north-west of the Acropolis, where family murders were tried.

Harry and I once clambered up the Areópagus many years ago. At the time I thought it a most extraordinary place to hold trials of any sort. To get up demanded risking life and limb on slippery steps cut into the rockface, and on the top there were many shallow hollows and uneven surfaces designed to send people sprawling. Climbing down from the Areópagus was a nightmare, and I would have fallen headlong had I not been helped by a strong young man who gave me his arm. Today, however, it is easy to do because a metal stairway like a fire-escape has been clamped to the rock, and a metal walkway encircles its summit. Perhaps in those earlier days of Orestes the Areópagus was flat without the erosions that have come with the passing of the centuries.

To continue with Orestes' trial. When the Athenian citizens have heard the prosecution and listened to his defence, lots are cast and the verdict is equally divided. Athena then casts the deciding vote and Orestes is acquitted.

The Furies (these irritating and persistent pricks of conscience) are incandescent with rage. They look on Athena as a goddess much younger than themselves, and for her to overrule their authority and acquit Orestes they regard as monstrous. Haven't they been the ones who first brought about a civilized society, they scream? But Athena assures them of their continued importance and, as a gesture of goodwill, bestows on them a cave on the north side of the Acropolis below her ancient temple.

What is more, she says, from now on they are to be known as the Eumenides (the 'kindly ones'). And so the Furies are soothed, and finally placated. How true it is that 'a soft word turns away wrath'!

Today their cave on the north side of the Acropolis is off-limits. I have tried to locate it from below, but trees and scrub conceal it. I was, however, assured by someone in authority that it definitely exists.

The fan-shaped amphitheatre of Dionysos Eleuthereus is open to visitors. It is small with tiered stone seats, though at the time of Socrates, the seats didn't exist and the audience sat on the sloping ground below the sheer-faced rock of the Acropolis. The semi-circular cream and grey flag-stones of the stage that you see today, and the long marble sculpted screen along the back, known as the *bema*, were not a feature at the time of Socrates either. Each marble panel of the *bema*, though, is thought to portray an episode from Dionysos' life.

Dionysos' birth, like that of the goddess Athena, was yet another strange, unlikely story. In it Zeus was captivated by Semele, the daughter of King Cadmus of Thebes.

When his wife Hera learned about his affair, in a jealous rage she persuaded Semele to ask Zeus to reveal himself to her in his full immortal glory on his next visit to her bed. This she did and, as Hera well knew, the blaze of Zeus' divinity immediately reduced the poor girl to a cinder. Zeus, however, rescued the embryo of his unborn child and placed it in his thigh till the infant was ready to be born.

Readers might well dismiss it as just another wild,

unlikely story. Yet, when archaeologists excavated King Cadmus' palace at Thebes (which today looks remarkably like a bombed-out site), they found an area which had been burned with such an intense and ferocious heat, greater than any normal fire, that it was felt there might be some truth to the legend.

Contemporary with Socrates was the tragic dramatist Euripides whose work Socrates particularly admired; it has even been suggested he helped write some of them. He certainly attended every Euripidean drama he could.

It is the popular belief that Euripides wrote his dramas in a cave up a mountain on the offshore island of Salamis. When I and two companions climbed the low mountain to visit it. We had to crouch down to get inside, then had to follow a narrow, unlit, winding passageway bent double. There was no light and my courage failed me, but my companion continued till she came to a low chamber where she could stand upright. Did Euripides really write his masterpieces in that cave? Or did he in fact work outside it where there was a flat grassy ledge beside a precipitous slope. There it was wonderfully isolated – a perfect escape for any serious writer, with the added bonus of a view to the Saronic gulf.

Like Socrates, Euripides was also known to question the truth of some stories of the gods, though by the time of Socrates' trial and execution he had taken himself off to Macedonia. He'd gone there at the invitation of King Archelaus who, envious of the renowned Greek culture at that time, wanted to enrich his own kingdom with such talent.

Euripides may have had religious doubts, but while in Macedonia he wrote a tragedy, the *Bacchae*, which suggests a conversion, or strong religious belief of some sort. As one of the characters in the play remarks, it is best not to *trifle with divinity*. Rather, you should respect the hallowed traditions that have been passed down ... *whatever subtleties this clever age invents*. Or, as Harry advises me repeatedly, it is better to go along with Christianity – to toe the line, and doff the cap – as you never know, it might be true.

Someone once said to me he only believed in the evidence of his eyes. Having given the words 'evidence of his eyes' some thought I, in my contrary way, realized suddenly there WAS evidence, and I found myself writing: 'Of course there is God! How can there be no God when there are so many priests and bishops of God? Are they priests and bishops of moonshine? Are they communing with vapour? Are the churches and cathedrals only built for the worship of gobbledegook? When the sign of the cross is made on a baby's brow at baptism, is the priest only a minister of bluff – because all the others have bluffed for over two thousand years?'

The City Dionysia festival was not just a contest for tragic dramatists, but for comic playwrights also. After three days of tragedy, it was time for laughter.

In 424 B.C. the comedian Aristophanes won first prize at the Lenaia festival. The young, humorous playwright's imaginative turn of mind catapulted him to the forefront of all other comic playwrights and, if any writer had a wild imagination and the capability of being a buffoon, it was Aristophanes.

Unlike the tragedians, Aristophanes never wrote about ancient myth and past historical events, but applied himself to topical subjects, frequently poking fun at the public figures of the day. No other playwright was better able to cut men down to size, and knock them off their pedestals.

It was Aristophanes' crazy comedy *Clouds* that caused a major stir having Socrates as the target of his wit. The plot revolves around a father who despairs of his son whose life is spent in gambling. Debts have accumulated and his father is determined to visit what is called the Thinkery where Socrates (unfairly classed in the play as a Sophist) will instruct him how to outwit his creditors who are clamouring for payment. True Sophists were trained in the art of persuasion, of being able to make a lie appear as truth – something Socrates was at pains to avoid. Only the absolute truth ever satisfied him.

Out of the Thinkery come two characters called Right and Wrong, known collectively as the Arguments. Wrong is confident he can persuade any Right-thinking citizen that he, Wrong, is the superior of the two.

In the comedy Socrates descends from the sky in a basket (by means of a theatrical prop, a machine known as a *mechane*). He has, he tells the audience, been studying the sun, and the stars, and declares that it is the clouds that produce rain, not Zeus (known as the 'cloud-gatherer'); and they, the clouds, also cause thunder, not Zeus. Such truths spoken in jest!

It is said that Socrates was in the audience and, on seeing himself as the butt of such humour, he rose and bowed to the audience seated on the ground around him. It is also said that Socrates made light of it and remarked calmly afterwards that, if what Aristophanes said about him was just, then he would try to reform himself, and if not, then it really didn't matter.

But it did matter. According to Plato in his *Apology* which he wrote as a record of Socrates' defence at his trial, Socrates spoke about those shadowy figures who ... *say that there is one Socrates...who ponders what is above the earth and investigates everything beneath it, and turns the weaker argument into the stronger...* Socrates at his trial was to say it was impossible to identify such unseen, invisible ill-wishers, quipping ...*except perhaps one who happens to be a comic playwright.*

Yet Socrates and Aristophanes were on friendly terms, though it was noted he wasn't present at his trial.

One might wonder what Aristophanes thought when he learned of Socrates' conviction and death. He was an avid reader and in all likelihood read Plato's *Apology*. If so, he may well have felt a sudden chill of remorse that Socrates had been condemned, in part due to ...*one who happens to be a comic playwright.* The butt of his crazy humour in *Clouds* had turned comedy to tragedy – laughter to tears.

I would like to end this chapter when I experienced a moment of profound drama which involved both the living and the dead.

Not so long ago in Athens, I and my two travelling companions at that time, noticed that the Bolshoi Ballet Company was performing at the Herodes Atticus theatre, south-west of the Acropolis. Ballet! A wordless off-shoot from the ancient dramas from the time of Socrates in the fifth century B.C.!

We bought the cheapest tickets (which were very

expensive at thirty pounds) in the highest tiered seats of this great Roman amphitheatre.

It was magnificent! The night was balmy, pigeons roosted in the Roman arches illuminated subtly by footlights around which moths flitted. Behind us was the floodlit Parthenon crowning the Acropolis.

But, oh, how I longed to have something to lean against! Somebody's knees were there, and I hoped whoever it was didn't mind me making use of them. In my discomfort on the tiered stone seat, the word 'enduring' the ballet was a better way of describing it, rather than 'enjoying it'. The ballet was a medley of dances, not any of the classics such as Swan Lake.

Long minutes of 'enduring' passed slowly till just before the interval. Then the principal male dancer began a long solo performance: leaping, arching his body backwards in mid-air, pirouetting and performing all the movements that male dancers can spectacularly achieve. He extended his body, arms and legs to the recording of Mozart's Theme from Concerto No. 21; there was no orchestra, only a piano recording which was being played slowly and profoundly, crescendoing gradually to *fortissimo* till the whole amphitheatre was suffused with its sublime sound.

My mind was filled with the overwhelming beauty of the moment: the velvety night sky and the floodlit ancient masterpieces of architecture.

A friend who used to visit us at the farm, was an amateur musician, and used to play this piece on our piano, each note played with extreme sensitivity. He had died quite suddenly that past year when only in his sixties – a severe heart-attack, the doctor had said. He'd died while doing what he loved best, playing his piano – possibly playing this same piece by Mozart which he did so exquisitely.

Seated there that night, watching this male dancer, and listening to the music, I felt overwhelmed like a drowning man whose joys and sorrows flash by – the death of the friend; Harry and the dog at home; our total devotion to each other; the tough times we'd been through while farming, and the freedom we now had as a result. All was reflected in this piano piece, and the arching, leaping, pirouetting dancer performing his solo act on stage that night below the Acropolis.

There could be nothing to follow that 'moment' that could equal it, and I didn't want to 'endure' what would come next as it could only be a lesser experience. For those sublime few minutes I'd quite forgotten the discomfort of my seat.

In the interval that followed, I told the others that the evening had been fantastic but I was going back to the hotel. They nodded understandingly.

"See you in the morning," I said.

Words said with such confidence! Maybe I should have added the two words 'I hope'. But that would have implied that there was a doubt – 'Hope', 'Doubt' – Socrates' laws of opposites. It is always better, even in death, to have hope. Hope for those who believe there's an afterlife; or hope for those who prefer the thought that you just go out like a light.

CHAPTER 3

PLATO'S *SYMPOSIUM*
APHRODITE, GODDESS OF LOVE

In Socrates' day there was no shame in gay relationships; in fact, it was expected that an older man should be attracted to an adolescent whom he could instruct and nurture with the knowledge he himself had acquired over the years.

It was well-known that Socrates had for long been attracted to Alcibiades, a handsome, blond and sexually attractive aristocrat. His father had died while he was still a child, and he'd been taken into the household of Pericles where he'd grown up alongside Pericles' sons who, according to all accounts, went off the rails much as Alcibiades was to.

In Plato's famous *Symposium* each guest is asked to speak on the delicate subject of Love with a capital L. In Socrates' day a symposium was a gathering of twenty or so men to celebrate some special event. They would eat and drink (the latter especially) and discuss some topic. Often there was entertainment, such as flute-girls, acrobats and suchlike. The guests would relax on couches arranged around the room, each one propped up on an elbow, with a hand free to raise his goblet of wine.

Before launching into Plato's *Symposium*, I will write briefly about one that Socrates attended which Xenophon, Socrates's former student and friend, describes in his *Memoirs*. In his report, Socrates is extraordinarily relaxed and cheerful. They have all just given their frank opinions on Beauty and homo-erotic Love, when suddenly Socrates remarks: *'As we're all so eager to have our voices heard… perhaps this would be the right moment to sing together.'* And with these words he started a song.

Not for a moment have I ever imagined Socrates singing – talking, yes, but singing? It is a cheerful spectacle of the great philosopher giving voice, joined, no doubt raucously, by the twenty or so other men present.

After the singing, Xenophon wrote how a dancing-girl had performed and was joined by a boy, and how Socrates had commented on their amazing agility: their ability to turn somersaults over sword-blades, for example, and how it was oddly disconcerting that they were able to bend their bodies into hoops. Then, in typical Socratean mode, his mind shoots off at the strangeness of certain facts which he's noticed. For instance, that a lamp will give light from its bright flame, whereas a bronze mirror, although bright, doesn't shed light, but shows the reflections of other things in itself. Similarly oil, which is liquid feeds the flame, but water which is also liquid, puts it out.

Such was Xenophon's first-hand report of Socrates enjoying himself at a symposium. Plato's *Symposium*, though, gives another insight into the character of Socrates.

★

Here in Plato's *Symposium*, the guests have eaten and drunk, and are completely relaxed. The party is taking place in the house of a tragic playwright Agathon. The year is 416 B.C., and Agathon has just won first prize at the Lenaia festival of drama so is celebrating with a symposium, together with his gay lover Pausanias.

The subject up for discussion is again Love, as it was at the one Xenophon described. It kicks off with Socrates' young friend Phaedrus giving examples of what he sees as pure Love. There is, for example, the legendary Love Alcestis showed for her husband King Admetus when she willingly sacrificed her life for him; or the deep Love Orpheus had for his wife Eurydice as he followed her down to Hades when she'd tragically died from a snake bite. The gods felt sorry for his grief so allowed her to return with him on one condition: that he did not look back at her as he led her out. Unfortunately, in his joy at retrieving her, he forgot the warning so lost her for ever.

Aristophanes is also at the gathering, and Plato writes how he cannot speak until he has been cured of hiccups – what else but a little comedy would we expect from this fun-loving playwright? He does what is advised by Erychimachus, a doctor who is present, and tickles his nose to make himself sneeze.

As ever, Aristophanes' contribution is a farcical spoof. Not for him is the creation story in the Old Testament which he might well have heard about, nor Plato's *Timaeus* which was an Egyptian creation story. No, Aristophanes' version is wildly imaginative. At the beginning of time, he says, men and women were attached back to back forming one big round body, each having four arms and four legs making eight appendages. In those far off days, he says, they could only move by cartwheeling like acrobats.

The reason for their circular shape, he asserts, is because they were descended from the sun, earth and moon. Their strength was terrifying, and they were highly ambitious and wanted to overthrow the Olympian gods. They were so dangerous, in fact, that Zeus felt obliged to call a council-meeting of the gods. After many discussions and much thought, Zeus decided the best solution was to cut each in half; this would not only weaken them, but benefit the gods as there would be more of them and, therefore, more worship and sacrificial offerings. If they then continued to behave outrageously, then he would halve them again and they'd have to go hopping around on one leg.

Aristophanes goes on to describe how the god Apollo was instructed to do the halving of them. Having performed this task, he had to twist every person's face and his halved neck around. To see their ghastly gash would jolt them into behaving much better – or at least more moderately – in the future. Apollo next pulled the skin all around their bodies to what we now call the stomach. And Aristophanes tells the guests to imagine a purse being closed by draw-strings. Where the skin was drawn together in a knot is what today we call the navel.

Because each halved body was once one, now they were separated there were males and females. Aristophanes' explanation for Love was that each (male or female) was constantly looking for his or her former half.

But! Because they'd been round and had been sliced in two, and their heads having had to be swivelled round towards the gash (now the stomach), their genitals were still on the original outer side, so they gradually began to die out. Zeus, realizing the problem, turned their genitals around and so intercourse was introduced, the man becoming the agent of generation taking place within the woman. And Aristophanes warns that if we humans are not to be split in half again and weakened still further, we must honour the gods and treat them with due reverence.

After this comical explanation of the human search for Love, the two following speeches – one by Agathon, the host of this symposium, followed by Socrates – pale into insignificance. I will, though, quote what Socrates was told by a woman named Diomita (thought to be a priestess) as it is very true of Socrates as you will see: ...*the beauties of the body are as nothing to the beauties of the soul*... *(Symposium: 210b)*

A sudden battering at the front-door interrupts the party, and Alcibiades arrives in a recklessly drunken state. He wears a bunch of ribbons on his head with which he intends to crown Agathon for his success in winning first prize at the Lenaia festival. There is a show of jealousy when he sees that Socrates, who makes room beside him, has been seated beside the handsome Agathon. Things settle down, however, when Socrates cheerfully admits his Love for Alcibiades. Taking centre stage, Alcibiades speaks about his own Love, even passion, for Socrates, and his helpless inability to guess what Socrates' true feelings really are. It is Socrates' unfathomable character which attracts him, he says, and if only he wasn't so drunk, he would call on the gods to witness the truth of what he is about to confess. The fact is his heart literally pounds and he even sheds tears when under the spell of Socrates' words. He has seen others too affected in the same way.

Is this emotion caused by Aphrodite, the goddess of Love, or by the god Eros, he wonders? In the *Symposium* they speak of Love with a capital L as being both male and female.

Here a short digression is needed to write a little about Aphrodite (female) whose son Eros (male) was said to be by Ares, god of war.

Aphrodite was married to Hephaestus, the lame son of Hera and Zeus, whose occupation was metal-work. That the beautiful Aphrodite was said occasionally to have been unfaithful to her lame and unattractive blacksmith of a husband is, perhaps, not too surprising.

The story of her love affair with Ares is well known, but I will relate it briefly here for those who do not know it. Her adultery was spotted by Helios (the sun) who then informed her husband. On hearing that his wife was routinely inviting Ares to her bed, Hephaestus devised a cunning plan. He created an invisible, fine-meshed golden net which he hung above the bed so that when his wife and Ares were next making love, the net descended over them and trapped them inescapably. Oh, the indignity of it! He then invited all the gods of Olympus to come and see the spectacle of the two caught in adultery; there was uproarious laughter at the sight of them. Some say that it was from their union that Eros was born – Eros, the mischief-maker, who was later portrayed with his bow and arrow which he fired at random, igniting men and women with instant passion. According to the poet Hesiod, though, Eros was born out of Chaos along with Tartarus (the Underworld) and Gaia (Mother Earth).

The best known version of Aphrodite's birth is of her rising from the waves off Paphos in Cyprus. This was because when Kronos castrated his father Ouranos (which I mentioned he did in Chapter 1), legend has it that he flung the genitals into the sea and the semen transformed into the goddess.

When we visited Paphos many years ago, I sat on the sea-shore alone one early morning, staring at a rock which was said to mark the exact spot where Aphrodite rose from the waves. I was actually staring at the wrong rock – 'You are in error', said a kindly German who was seated nearby but staring at another rock. What did it really matter!

There in Cyprus, according to Greek legend, she fell madly in love with the beautiful young Adonis. Tragically, Adonis was killed by a wild boar whilst out hunting in the forests, and Aphrodite was left distraught and heart-broken. One story has it that it was the cuckolded Hephaestus who set the wild boar on Adonis out of pique at Aphrodite's infidelity, others that it was Ares out of jealousy.

While on Cyprus we followed what was popularly called the Aphrodite Trail along a rocky peninsula (the Akamas peninsula). We had with us a stalwart, down-to-earth friend whom we affectionately called the Stoic because she'd had a tough life, yet nothing ever got her down. She lived on Cyprus, was eager to see more of the legendary side of it, and was excellent at keeping things harmonious between Harry and me when I was pushing my luck too far.

Not long after starting the trail we found ourselves at what was known as Aphrodite's Grotto. It was about ten in the morning but we were already hot despite the short walk. We sat down beside the clear, aquamarine pool fed by a spring, and watched the water trickle and drip down the surrounding rocks. Bamboos grew around the spot, and a fig tree hung its boughs over it. There was nothing but the sound of water and doves cooing (sacred to Aphrodite).

It was a place for deep-felt emotion and amorous advances, but Harry didn't rise to the occasion. As we were the only ones there, I took off my sandals and dipped my feet into the cold water, defying a notice forbidding it, to which Harry said he thought by the look of my toes I could do with a spell at the chiropodist. Chiropodist? I looked at my feet with renewed interest, and saw at once they weren't exactly those of a young nymph, but they got me around.

Where was this thing called Love? Years of marriage and farming hadn't exactly done much for romance. But love has many facets like a diamond, and to expect the love of youth to persist is the first obstacle to be overcome by the average married couple. Love changes, just as humans do as they battle their way through life: through careers, babies, teenage offspring and retirement; through the tough times and the moments of plain sailing.

Chiropodist or no, my feet served me well as we began the long trudge up a rocky path amongst stunted pines. Every now and then we reached vantage points high above the sea, where we were able to look down over inlets and small coves where the water was like green shot-silk, or shades of sapphire and turquoise.

The trail took us higher and higher and then, after an hour, began to descend, until we came finally to a magnificent glade with a huge old oak tree and a spring. This was known as the Shelter of the Queen. It was here, so it is said, that Aphrodite rested after bathing in her Grotto. It was shadowy and cool under the branches, an oasis of charm after the scorched rocky track. A welcome breeze blew gently, soughing through the branches of the surrounding tall pine trees.

Was this where Aphrodite and Adonis first made love? It was certainly a place to linger and relax.

I wanted to walk on up to the crest of the next rocky peak to see what lay beyond.

"Be it on your own head," said the Stoic ominously, whose short, damp hair clung around her amiable face like a bathing-cap. Harry was seated on the ground and wasn't going anywhere, so I set out alone.

I strode up the track keeping an eye out for snakes and, in order to achieve my goal, I kept up the pace higher and higher until wham! A sudden whirling of the senses, and the rocks seemed to spin around. I was suddenly faced with the fact that I was mortal. To be unable to continue was a new experience.

I was on the border-line of the great divide, between life and death, and gathering the gods to me. I managed to stagger to the shelter of a stunted fir, drank from my bottle of water but wanted to be sick.

Harry hadn't been happy about my trek into the heat where the sun's rays bounced back off the rocks; he'd been watching my progress and now my lack of it. When he saw I was stretched out flat, he came to the rescue. This was love!

When Harry reached me, he more or less carried me back to the cool shelter of the glade. I lay out on the ground while the others discussed my predicament as though I wasn't there.

"She's obviously dehydrated," said the Stoic. "It can be fatal if not treated. I imagine she hasn't done this before?"

"She saw the doctor because she had dizzy spells last year," Harry said. "He didn't seem to panic."

"They're not paid to panic," said the Stoic.

I began to feel hungry and asked for a marmite sandwich and a banana. These were brought to me promptly from our picnic box, and I realized there were some benefits in being ill.

"Your wife is on the mend," said the Stoic. "If we wait till later, I think she'll manage the walk back."

"Don't fuss. I'm fine really," I said.

"No, we won't fuss," said the Stoic. "Here, drink some more water," and she put a hand under my head and helped me to sit up. "And eat these salted peanuts," she commanded. And she wet a cloth from the spring and plonked it on my forehead, and told me not to argue but to do as I was told for once.

Several hours later, with the Stoic fanning my face and Harry holding my arm, we ventured out into the late afternoon sun. "We're not fussing," repeated the Stoic, "only trying to make sure you make it to the road. We've two or three kilometres. How are you feeling?"

"I'm all right for the moment," I said, totally unsure of myself.

There were narrow tracks where the rocks fell away steeply which I manoeuvred past on all fours. Then Harry took my arm and the Stoic fanned my face, and we carried on, putting on an act of jolly camaraderie and smiling as other hikers passed us. Every twenty or thirty paces the Stoic called a halt and I was ordered to rest.

By the time we reached Aphrodite's Grotto again, I was feeling almost normal.

"Almost normal, she says. That's bad news for us!" the Stoic said. "She'll be wanting us to gallivant off somewhere else in no time!"

To get back to Plato's *Symposium*, Socrates and Love!

Alcibiades continues his inebriated reminiscences, telling Socrates that he is the only person in the world in whose company he's felt something which people would think he was incapable of feeling – shame. So long as he is with him he is full of good intentions but, as soon as he is out of his presence he gets seduced by the acclaims of the masses. He feels shame because of the promises he has made, but never keeps when Socrates is absent.

Alcibiades complains miserably that, although Socrates has all the appearances of being in love with him, he is annoyingly *chock-full of self-control.*

And Alcibiades makes a full confession of his own passion, and the attempts he has made to seduce him. He describes how he once planned an evening alone with the great man, but was disappointed because nothing happened; how he next invited him to the gymnasium where they'd exercised together (probably in the nude), and even wrestled together, often with no one else around. Does he have to spell it out, he asks in despair? He got precisely nowhere with him.

Thoroughly frustrated by his unrequited love (he is only used to adoration and instant sexual gratification), Alcibiades tells them how he then invited Socrates to dine alone with him, and his invitation was accepted. It was, he says, as if he himself was the older lover and Socrates the boy he had designs on. To his bitter disappointment, Socrates left immediately after the meal. He asked him again, and this time kept him talking late into the night. When Socrates eventually prepared to leave, Alcibiades persuaded him to stay because of the lateness of the hour. So he settled down to sleep on the couch where he'd been seated at dinner – and Alcibiades confesses he is probably only speaking frankly now because of the wine but, as he understands they are supposed to be speaking the truth, so it would be wrong to pass over Socrates' awe-inspiring behaviour. At the time he'd felt, he says, like someone who'd been bitten by a snake – or something even more excruciating as, to put it candidly, it couldn't have attacked a more vulnerable part of his body. With Socrates lying close to him, his frustrated passion reached such a fever-pitch, that he eventually asked Socrates if he was asleep.

"No, far from it," came the reply. And Alcibiades speaks of the conversation they then had. How he'd said to Socrates that he thought he was in love with him; that, he thought Socrates was the only lover he had ever desired who was good enough for him, but he, Socrates, was too shy to admit it. So now he was going to tell him exactly how he felt – he believed it would be stupid not to gratify Socrates in what he was certain he too wanted. The fact was that he thought also there was nothing more important than to become as good a person as possible under Socrates' guidance.

To this Socrates apparently replied with his usual good humour, remarking that if Alcibiades' opinion of him were right and he was able to make him a better person, then what he was saying was that Alcibiades wanted to give him his beautiful body in return for Socrates' ugly one with its inner beauty. That being the case, then he reckoned Alcibiades would benefit far more than he would: *"a real gold for bronze exchange you're planning,"* was Socrates' frank comment. And with those words Alcibiades was left totally defeated. In despair, that night he told Socrates that he must be the one to decide what was best for them both under the circumstances, to which Socrates had replied cheerfully that he thought that an excellent idea. *"From now on we'll put our heads together and do whatever seems best."*

Oh, how frustrating Socrates could be!

After his confession of Love for him that night, Alcibiades tells the guests how, in desperation, he went and lay down beside Socrates and put his arms around him *...this remarkable, wonderful man – he is, you know – and I lay there with him all night long*. And Alcibiades challenges

Socrates to deny the truth of what he has been recounting. He even calls on the gods to witness the truth of what he's been telling them. And Alcibiades goes on to confess that he might as well have been sleeping with his father or brother *for all the naughtiness we got up to.*

I once tackled a vicar I happened to be sitting beside at a wedding reception, who said in response to some query I must have made, that the greatest of things was Love. I had probably drunk too much champagne, but I immediately asked him what he meant by Love? The word had so many connotations. You can love sausages, love adulterously, love to laugh, love to go on holiday. So what exactly does 'the greatest of things is Love' mean?

Hum. Haw. Hum.

He threw the question back at me. "What do you think is the most important thing in life?" he asked. Surprising myself as much as I probably surprised him, I said, 'Duty'. 'If everybody stopped talking about Love and did what they knew was their duty, the world would surely be a better place?' I was in full flow. 'Love is something you either feel or you don't. You can't discipline yourself to love something if you're revolted by it – tolerate it, yes, but love it, no.'

Hum. Haw. Hum.

So that just about wraps up Alcibiades' speech on Love. It seems a great pity that for one who had so many advantages in life: good looks, wealth, an aristocratic background, and with Socrates doing all he could to turn around his hopelessly erratic character, that Socrates was eventually to see the downfall of his young, intelligent and gifted protégé.

His disgrace began when, on the eve of an all-important naval campaign which Alcibiades commanded, many statues of the god Hermes (known as Hermae) were found mutilated, and Alcibiades and his drunken friends were suspected of their desecration. It didn't bode well for the expedition he was to lead. It set sail on its mission anyway but failed completely to achieve its goal.

So what were these Hermae? They were marble or stone uprights topped by the bearded smiling head of the god Hermes, many having on them an erect phallus. Hermes, son of Zeus and the nymph Maia, was messenger-god, and protector of travellers. Because of this a Herm stood at many cross-roads, and outside private houses.

Alcibiades was also believed to have abused the Eleusian Mysteries of Demeter by play-acting them before his friends – a highly sacrilegious betrayal since all initiates were sworn to absolute secrecy.

Socrates must have been sadly disappointed when this favourite Adonis-like, beautiful yet depraved young man of his, a man with such potential, fell from grace. He was in due course exiled, then defected to the Spartans in the Peloponnesean War, and even served the Persians for a while, before he was finally assassinated in 404 B.C.

When Socrates came to trial five years later, his association with Alcibiades was to weigh heavily against him.

CHAPTER 4

PLATO'S *APOLOGY*
THE LAW COURT AND SOCRATES' TRIAL

By the spring of 399 B.C., Athens had fallen from her pinnacle of greatness and was suffering severe hardships. To explain briefly: She had been defeated by Sparta in the on-off thirty-year Peloponnesian War, been ravaged by the plague, and had endured the brief and murderous rule of what became known as the Thirty Tyrants (though democracy had soon been reinstated). Clearly the gods were wrathful and a scapegoat was required. Who better than Socrates? Wasn't it he who asked questions concerning the truth of the stories regarding them? Didn't Socrates converse with young men, corrupting their minds under his influence? A persistent speaker, constantly to be heard arguing in the Agora about topics to see if there was any truth to the accepted facts?

Xenophon once overheard Socrates questioning Critias and Charicles (two of the hated Thirty Tyrants) after an edict had been brought in by them forbidding Socrates from conversing with young men. Socrates promptly asked them what they meant exactly by 'not conversing'? Charicles was annoyed that he could pretend to be so dense. Best not to talk to the young at all, if he was to be so stupid, he'd snapped back. Undeterred, Socrates persisted. To avoid any misunderstanding, could he tell him what age he considered young, he enquired?

To this the already nettled Charicles replied through gritted teeth that anyone immature, such as young men too young to serve on the council – the age of thirty, for instance.

Socrates then wanted to know whether he could ask someone under thirty what the price of some article was if he wanted to buy it? Or, if a young man under the age of thirty were to ask him a question to which he knew the answer, such as where Charicles lived, or where Critias lived, was he not to reply? 'Yes, of course he could', came the brusque and increasingly impatient retort. Socrates knew how to needle people whom he considered petty-minded!

So Socrates is in court. As he sees it, his 'inner voice' has brought him to this point in his life where he is standing trial. His prosecutors have taken their oath before the gods, standing by the six-foot oblong oath-stone (the *lithos*), as has each member of the jury also. The oath-stone stands in the Agora before the columned Stoa Basileios where the court proceedings are being held. And some fifty metres beyond is the Altar of the Twelve Gods. The immortal eyes are watching and guiding events. Each juryman in court will do his duty according to the will of the gods.

The trial has started, and Socrates' three prosecutors have spoken, one of whom is the youthful Meletus whom Socrates is known to have described as having straight

CHAPTER FOUR 53

hair, not much of a beard, and a long nose.

There are as many as five hundred jurors in court, all of whom have been listening to the prosecution. Amongst the onlookers is the young Plato himself, a devoted follower of Socrates.

It is now Socrates' turn to speak in his own defence. He makes no attempt to persuade the jury of his innocence. He addresses them as his fellow citizens, and wonders what their opinion is regarding what they have just heard. For his part he thinks his prosecutors have been very persuasive, though hardly a word of what they have said he considers to be true. What is more, he thinks that they should take note of the warning by his prosecutors that they, the jury, should be careful not to be taken in by anything he says as he is a clever speaker. What, though, do they mean by 'clever', he wonders? If they are implying that he speaks the truth then, yes, he is a positive orator!

Socrates' confidence in himself is entirely due to what he believes is God's guidance, because God cannot be wrong, he insists. To disobey his God because he fears conviction and death is quite out of the question.

If the jury thinks he should feel ashamed of standing there in court, then they are mistaken because he knows he has never said or done anything he has not considered to be good and right. He is, therefore, quite ready to accept death since it was his God who first brought him to philosophy and his present state. And Socrates emphasizes that as long as he lives he will continue to practise philosophy and exhort his listeners to lead good and just lives. He implores them as citizens of Athens not to aim for wealth and power but to pay regard to the state of their souls.

Once in full flow, there is no stopping Socrates, except the water-clock which is running out of time. But Socrates for the moment is unstoppable: *...I believe that no greater good has ever befallen you in our city than my service to my god, because all I do is to go about persuading you, young and old alike, not to care for your bodies or for your wealth so intensely as for the greatest well-being of your souls... (Apol. 30a)*

Socrates himself was decidedly unmaterialistic. He set an example of frugality and simplicity, as Alcibiades pointed out in Plato's *Symposium*, by possessing only one cloak which he wore summer and winter, and going about barefoot.

Socrates was never judgemental but treated everyone with good humour and affection. He loved Athens and what she stood for, but abhorred the fact she had overreached herself when greed and riches had gone to her head. He wasn't politically minded, but intensely interested in philosophy – the love of wisdom ('philo' in Greek meaning 'to love', and 'sophia' meaning 'wisdom').

Socrates had gained a reputation for wisdom after a certain Chaerephon (an admirer of his) enquired of the Delphic oracle whether there was anybody wiser than Socrates. To this the oracle had replied that there wasn't.

Socrates tells the court how he was genuinely mystified that the oracle had said there was no one wiser than him. He reminds the jury of the occasion, and how he had subsequently gone around questioning at length anyone who had a reputation for wisdom and who invariably thought himself wise too, only to discover he was not at all. In that way, he confesses, he became disliked by them and their admirers, many of whom he expects are in the jury that day. However, having questioned these 'wise men', he began to think that the Delphic oracle had undoubtedly been right and he was wiser, since he knew he knew nothing, and the others thought they knew everything.

The time Socrates has had to present his defence has finally run out, and the jurors give their verdict. Each has been given two metal discs, one pierced and the other not; they must now decide whether to drop the pierced one into the ballot box for guilty, or the unpierced for innocent.

It is done, and Socrates is found guilty. It is what he expected. His sentence will be either exile, a hefty fine, or execution. But he is allowed one more opportunity to speak. He is allowed to state what penalty he himself thinks he should be given. After that the jury will give its final verdict.

He is expected to plead his innocence; or even to bring his young sons before the jury to reduce everyone in court to tears and compassion. Not a bit of it. No, instead of pleading innocence, Socrates says cheerfully that he is not surprised at the court's decision though, had a mere thirty votes gone the other way, he would have been acquitted.

So what alternative penalty does he think should be imposed on him? Well, obviously it should be one he really believes he deserves. Since all his life he's tried to persuade them all to lead moral lives, he regards himself as the city's benefactor. *Well then, what IS fitting for a poor man who is a benefactor, and who needs time free for exhorting you? Nothing could be more fitting, fellow Athenians, than to give such a man regular free meals in the Prytaneum. (Apology 36d)*

What a nerve! Ever jocular, Socrates thinks, he deserves the same award as winners at the Olympic Games who receive free meals for life in the Prytaneum.

The Prytaneum is the political centre of Athens, where the eternal flame of Hestia, goddess of the hearth and home, burns continually, representing the symbolic heart of the city.

Hestia is a seldom heard of goddess but was of major importance. She was a virgin goddess, never quarrelsome as were the other gods and goddesses. She was at the heart of family and civic life, and every household had a hearth consecrated to her, as did every city Prytaneum. With the founding of a new colony, a flame from her sacred hearth in Athens would be taken to light the hearth in the Prytaneum of the new colony.

Hestia, along with Zeus, was at the heart of the Olympic Games. Legend has it that Zeus threw a thunderbolt from Mt. Olympus and, where it landed in the far west of the Peloponnese, marked the location for the Games.

The whole area around where the thunderbolt landed was then dedicated to Zeus, and the spot honoured with an altar dedicated to him. At first the altar had been relatively small, but in time it became a significant landmark with a perimeter base of a hundred and twenty-five feet, requiring ramps up which the sacrificial cattle were driven to a platform on its summit; the reason being that the ash from previous sacrifices – a hundred bullocks (a hecatomb) on each occasion – was never removed.

Were those who witnessed the death of these animals unaffected by it? We once attended a festival which celebrated the feast-day of Sts. Constantine and Helena (Constantine's mother), when a sect known as the Anastenaria marked the occasion by walking barefoot through fire, having first sacrificed a bull. Wanting to see the fire-walkers, I was determined also to be an eye-witness to an actual bull-sacrifice which had been such a part of life in ancient Greece. I steeled myself for the occasion.

The bull's horns were decorated with red ribbons, and it was tied up to a railing, away from the milling crowd.

Two men in rubber aprons were making ready, and there was no one else present. One of the men started sharpening a long knife, and while he was doing it the bull raised his handsome head and made eye contact with me. Oh, hello! It then lowered its head again so was concealed by the men; I could only see its solid body – a lovely healthy animal. A moment passed and suddenly the body slumped to earth with a heavy thud: the deed was done. I might have accepted its death calmly if its hind hoof hadn't begun to claw the ground frantically, before finally lying still. At that point the fine line between life and death hit me – or maybe it was the struggle for life as its leg clawed at the ground trying to gain strength to rise to its former dignified self as a bull. A lump rose to my throat and I failed hopelessly to control myself. I gave a great sob and tears welled and coursed down my cheeks.

Harry, who'd tried to persuade me against watching, had been keeping an eye out. When he saw me turn away with bowed head and a hand searching for something to mop myself up with, he came quickly with a handerchief. "Not the end of the world, old thing," he said. But it was the end of the world! and his words brought on renewed sobs.

To continue with Olympia for a moment. It was during Socrates' lifetime that a remarkable new temple of Zeus was built there in Zeus' honour. It had massive columns and a roof tiled in Pentelic marble. The great sculptor Phidias (responsible for the Parthenon marbles and the cult statue of Athena there) created within the temple here a gargantuan cult statue of Zeus seated on a throne. He was portrayed with a winged Nike (representing victory) perched on the palm of one hand, and a sceptre topped by an eagle (his symbol) in the other.

Zeus was at the very heart of the ritual that went with

the Olympic Games. At the opening of them, everyone involved came to the Bouleuterion (the Council House there) and swore an oath before an altar and statue of Zeus, that they wouldn't cheat or bribe, and would observe the rules of the Games.

On the last day of the Olympic Games, a grand procession of judges, administrators and priests, together with the winner of each event came to stand before Zeus in this his new temple. Each victorious athlete wore a fillet of wool around his head, and carried a palm branch in his right hand. It wasn't until his name was called out by the herald, that he received his award and was crowned with a simple wreath of wild olive. It was a form of communion with Zeus, and an acknowledgement that he (the victor) had received the god's divine favour and patronage. Then, on his return to Athens (if that was his city) he was fêted and, as recognition of his national stature, was awarded free meals for life.

We have come way off track from Socrates in court!

Having cheerfully announced what he thinks he deserves as Athens' benefactor – in other words he should be treated as an Olympic champion would be – he goes on to say that he could suggest alternative penalties, such as a long imprisonment, a fine or banishment, but he considers such a fate to be worse than death at his time of life.

And so Socrates gives himself over to what they the jury decide should be his fate. If he is condemned to death, he tells them, it will be those who vote for his execution who will stand condemned to injustice as judged by Truth. Just as he will accept his penalty, so must they accept their guilt. But, he adds cheerfully, he imagines it's all for the best.

And for those who voted for his acquittal? He assures them that it was his 'inner voice' which has brought him to this moment. Since it never opposed him at any point in his trial, whereas it had formerly always intervened when he was doing the wrong thing, he accepts whatever they decide.

As for death. Well, if it is anything like being in a deep sleep, then it is nothing to be afraid of. Or, alternatively, if death is merely taking a trip to some other place then how wonderful to meet such people as Orpheus, Homer or King Agamemnon, and to ask them such questions as who amongst them they think wise, or thinks himself to be wise and isn't.

Good naturedly, Socrates says, he bears no ill-will towards those who have condemned him. He asks them only to see to it that if his three sons grow up to care for money or anything else more than goodness, or they begin to think too highly of themselves, then they are to be reproved.

And his final words are: *But enough. It is now time to leave – for me to die, and for you to live – though which of us has the better destiny is unclear to everyone, save only to God.* (Apol. 42a)

And so Socrates accepts his fate with equanimity, and is led from the Law Court to the nearby prison for execution. He cannot, though, be put to death immediately because it is April and a ship has just set sail on its annual sacred mission to Delos, birthplace of Apollo. During its absence, it is the law that no executions are permitted. So while we wait, I will write about the all important god Apollo and his twin sister Artemis.

… OH, SOCRATES!

CHAPTER 5

APOLLO AND HIS TWIN SISTER ARTEMIS

Before writing about Apollo, I must first explain why there was an annual sacred mission to Delos. The reason went back to the time King Minos ruled Crete when he did a shameful thing. He wanted to sacrifice a bull to Poseidon, god of the sea, but could find no animal from his own herd worthy of the god. Poseidon, therefore, presented the king with his own fine bull to sacrifice to him. However, King Minos thought it too good to kill, so he sacrificed one of his own after all.

His prize bull withheld? This greatly angered Poseidon who immediately caused Pasiphae, King Minos' wife, to develop a passion for the creature which resulted in the unseemly birth of the Minotaur, half-man, half-bull. The disgrace of it caused King Minos to hide it away in a Labyrinth out of sight of prying eyes.

Without going into details of the whys and wherefores, at a later date Poseidon's bull was brought to mainland Greece where one of the sons of King Minos was killed by it. At the time Aegeus was king of Athens, and King Minos blamed him for the death of his son. He, therefore, demanded compensation in the form of a yearly tribute of seven youths and seven maidens whose bodies he then fed to the Minotaur.

When King Aegeus' son, Theseus, was old enough, he was determined to stop this tragic waste of young life. So one year he volunteered to be one of the fourteen, with the intention of killing the monster and so putting an end to the yearly tribute once and for all. Before setting off on his dangerous mission, however, he swore an oath to Apollo that, if successful in his enterprise, he would send a sacred ship to holy Delos annually – holy because it was on Delos (a tiny island in the Cyclades) that Apollo was born.

As luck would have it, on Theseus' arrival at the palace of King Minos, Ariadne (the king's daughter) fell passionately in love with him. In order to save his life she gave him a ball of golden thread to unwind as he entered the Labyrinth so, once he'd killed the Minotaur, he was able to retrace his steps by following the thread out again.

Theseus' mission was a success, and Ariadne sailed away with him to the island of Naxos; there they lived happily for a while till immortal Dionysos appeared on the scene. As soon as he set eyes on the beautiful Ariadne, Dionysos was overcome by desire, and Theseus had to leave. By then anyway it was high time to fulfil the oath he'd sworn to Apollo, and to return to his royal duties as heir to the throne.

On his way back to Athens, Theseus stopped off at Delos to pay his respects to the god. While there, he founded the Delian Games which consisted of athletics, horse-racing and musical contests. He also introduced what was to become known as the Crane dance, a sinewy, serpentining movement which represented the winding passage of the Minotaur's Labyrinth. The Games and the

Crane dance became part of the annual celebrations.

On the arrival at Delos of the sacred ship from Athens – and it is said that the ship at the time of Socrates was the very one Theseus had sailed on – the envoys walked in procession to the temple of Apollo, singing a hymn recounting the story of the birth of Apollo and his divine twin sister Artemis, the virgin goddess of hunting. They intoned chants in honour of Apollo whilst making a solemn tour of the sanctuary of the god. After offering sacrifice, the Delian Games began, and the sacred Crane dance was performed before the altar of Apollo.

The story of Apollo's birth is another weird and wonderful one. In it Zeus loved the immortal Titaness Leto who became pregnant with twins by him. In a fury Hera forbade any place under the sun to allow Leto to give birth on its soil.

With Leto's confinement imminent, Zeus turned for help to his brother Poseidon. As luck would have it, Poseidon knew of a tiny, submerged island which was drifting aimlessly with no purpose to its existence; at the time it was known as A-delos, meaning 'invisible'. Poseidon raised the island and anchored it with diamond chains to the sea-bed; from then on it was called Delos (meaning 'manifest').

The island, though, also feared Hera's wrath and, not until Leto swore an oath on the river Styx (the greatest oath immortals could take), that after the birth she would build a temple on Delos, and it would become the most revered island in the Hellenic world, did Delos consent to the birth taking place on her territory.

The island's fame spread far and wide, thanks to Leto fulfilling her vow; even today pilgrims come by the boatload from all over the world; so many, in fact, that visitors are allowed a few hours there only.

When Harry and I made the journey, it was the light that first struck me as our small boat approached – a decided lustre that seemed to shine around it. Not only was it the light but, as we drew nearer, dolphins arched in and out of the waves – dolphins were sacred to Apollo, and to me it seemed they'd been sent by the god to welcome us.

It is said that Leto's confinement lasted nine days, and during that time she clung to a palm tree close by what has become known as the Sacred Lake (now dry). A solitary palm was clearly visible as our boat sailed in – surely planted there to excite visitors?

The story regarding the nativity of Apollo is that Hera, forever resentful of the impending birth, kept Eileithyia, goddess of childbirth, well away on Mt. Olympus. But after nine days had passed, Iris, goddess of the rainbow, was bribed with a gold necklace to fetch Eileithyia to help poor suffering Leto with her protracted travail.

According to Homer's *Hymn to Apollo*, when Apollo was born ...*all Delos blossomed with gold, as when a hilltop is heavy with woodland flowers, beholding the child of Zeus and Leto...* He was wrapped in swaddling-clothes and fed nectar and ambrosia (the food of the gods). But the swaddling-clothes could not contain the infant, and he burst forth from them, crying: ... *"May the harp and the bending bow be my delight, and I shall prophesy to men the unerring will of Zeus."...*

It's easy to get lost in the maze of ancient ruins on Delos but, at the centre of this tiny island, are three massive, well-worn marble steps marking the entrance to the great sanctuary of Apollo. Three Doric columns and a rectangular outline of large stone blocks are all that remain of his temple. Entering the so-called portal it is possible to stand at its centre and remember its remarkable history. It is there in the temple, that the Greek city states (members of the Delian League), once held their meetings; there too that the treasury had been kept, until Pericles cunningly persuaded the members of the Delian League that Athens would serve the purpose more conveniently – more profitably was more like it.

While there, Harry and I climbed Mt. Cynthos, the highest point on Delos. On our way, rather surprisingly, we passed a temple of Hera. After all she'd done to obstruct the birth of Apollo, it was strange that she was honoured here on Apollo's island. Perhaps, however, the inhabitants felt it prudent to appease her wrathful, jealous nature. There was a stepped path to help us climb up the steep slope of Cynthos. The *meltemi* (a persistent strong northerly wind) was cooling but battered the senses. Near the summit, we managed with care, despite the force of the gale, to sit down on a rock. We were in the location of a temple of Zeus and another of Athena. Whatever had once been up there was mostly blown away, leaving only the odd marble column-drum.

It was again from Mt. Cynthos that the light struck me as we gazed out over the island – a wonderful pure, bright sheen extending over the mushroom-grey of the island, accentuating its white marble ruins. The surrounding sea glittered in shades of turquoise and sapphire, flecked with white crested waves. Here and there a white cruise-liner could be seen sailing in, bringing more visitors, so fulfilling the oath sworn by Leto that the island's former rocky barrenness would turn to riches as a result of the birth of Apollo.

Three hours allowed only! What a rush! There was no time to loiter in a relaxed way. As it was, when we eventually hurried back to our boat, the captain was already shading his eyes, watching out for his last two passengers who were by then running along the dusty track towards him.

We mumbled our apologies, and stayed on deck to watch the boat draw away from the island. We had all the time in the world now that we were sailing away. The lustre and sparkle of that solitaire diamond gradually disappeared as the deep blue sea began to toss the boat on the white crested waves. The *meltemi* was relentless. Oooooh! Aaaaah! We staggered to the companionway and went down to the warmth of the cabin; there I took out my notebook and scribbled: 'It was the light that first struck me...'

Enough then of Delos. It is now time to relate how Apollo's famous oracle site at Delphi came to be founded.

Homer's same *Hymn to Apollo* continues from Apollo's birth on Delos to his extensive journeying by sea till he comes to Delphi. Homer relates how merchants (some say pirates) were sailing to Pylos from Crete in a black-prowed galley when Apollo, disguised as a dolphin (yes, a dolphin, which is why they are sacred to him), leapt from the sea and landed on the deck. This was regarded as ...*a portent great and terrible.* Apollo then used his immortal powers to guide the galley towards the coast close to his intended site and then ...*like a star at high noon, while the gledes of fire flew from him, and the splendour flashed to the heavens...he soared from the boat and descended to his sanctuary, which till then had been sacred to Gaia* (Mother Earth).

Socrates, of course, would have known Homer's hymn and the legends attached to the oracular site. He would have known that the first thing Apollo did when he arrived was to kill the Python/Dragon. Homer calls it a 'dragoness', and his description of her death-throes is vivid: ... *writhing in strong anguish, and mightily panting she lay, rolling about the land. Dread and dire was the din, as she writhed hither and thither through the wood, and gave up the ghost.*

The Delphic landscape is a dramatic one. Apollo's temple, with its seven remaining upright columns, stands on a terrace in the foothills of Mt. Parnassus in perfect harmony with its awe-inspiring surroundings of mountain peaks and ravines. The Sacred Way winds up from the Castalian spring beside the main Athens-Delphi highway at the foot of the twin Phaedriades rocks. There, water cascades down a crevice between the rocks into a paved area where petitioners once purified themselves, before following the Sacred Way to Apollo's temple.

At the heart of the temple, the Pythia (Apollo's priestess) sat on a tripod set over a cavity in the ground in the *adyton*, the holy of holies. The Pythia was so-named after the Python/dragon Apollo slew. She was given laurel leaves to chew and, from the vapours that rose from the cavity over which she sat in a trance-like state, she became inspired to speak. It was through her only that Apollo delivered his answers to questions such as to marry or not, to go to war or not, to colonize or not, and so on. When I say Apollo, it was generally thought it was Zeus speaking through his son.

Gifts presented to Apollo by the islands, colonies and individuals in gratitude for the oracle's help and guidance, flanked the Sacred Way. People came from far and wide to consult Apollo with their problems, hoping through

Apollo's Pythia, his priestess, to be guided on the right road to success and happiness.

Many famous legendary names from antiquity are known to have come with their diverse problems: King Oedipus, for example, who wanted to know who his true parents were, and who learned alarmingly from the oracle that one day he would murder his father and marry his mother. Or Theseus' father, King Aegeus, who remained childless despite two marriages, and came in desperation for advice – the conundrum he received from the Pythia was baffling; nevertheless he fathered Theseus soon afterwards. Then there was the hapless Orestes, son of King Agamemnon, who was told to avenge his father's death, and to murder his mother, resulting in the awakening of the dreaded Furies who, from then on, were to torment and harass him without mercy.

A curious response, and one that racked the brains of those responsible for the defence of Athens against the Persians, was: ...*Zeus of the broad heaven gives to the Tritoborn a wooden wall, alone to remain undestroyed, and it will bless you and your children.*

Armed with this problematic response, the envoys returned to Athens where those in command scratched their heads, some thinking the wooden wall must be the palisade around the Acropolis, and others that it could indicate the wooden triremes of the Greek fleet. The latter proved to be correct. At any rate, the ships set sail, and the Persian fleet was soundly defeated at the famous Battle of Salamis 480 B.C.

The last oracular pronouncement from the Pythia at Delphi was to Julian the Apostate who had sent an envoy enquiring about Christianity: *Tell the king, the fairwrought hall has fallen to the ground. No longer has Phoebus* (Apollo) *a hut, nor a prophetic laurel, nor a spring that speaks. The water of speech even is quenched.* Some say the response was a deliberate pious fraud, a ruse to promote the Christian faith. True or false, it worked as Christianity triumphed.

Before leaving Delphi, we mustn't forget the two famous maxims inscribed on the walls of the temple: 'Know thyself' and 'Nothing in excess'. In other words, do not attempt what is beyond your capabilities, and moderate your needs since there's no advantage to be gained in unnecessary indulgence: two things Socrates tried to instil into the young men he conversed with. If female readers wonder why women seldom seem to be mentioned where Socrates is concerned, it is because women in those days were kept well in the background – family and the home were their province. Nevertheless, Socrates is reported to have said: 'Once made equal to man, woman becomes his superior'. To which I would add a word of warning to women from Apollo's maxim: 'Nothing in excess'.

Any attentive reader might remember that Apollo had a twin sister. Artemis was goddess of the hunt and defender of wild animals, all weak things and children. Like her half-sister Athena she was a virgin goddess. She was later identified with the moon, thus eclipsing the seldom-heard-of moon-goddess Selene. This, of course, balanced well with Apollo who was identified with the sun: Phoebus Apollo, as he was often referred to, 'phoebos' meaning 'radiant', 'pure', 'light'.

Artemis is thought to have been born before Apollo. It is questionable where; some say just before Apollo on Delos, while others say it was at Ortygia (west of Greece).

In the latter story she was born a week before Apollo, and then helped her mother Leto across the sea to Delos and actually assisted her with Apollo's birth – hence her being goddess of young things.

Artemis is on the whole remembered as a goddess of the hunt. Her characteristics are conflicting as she is both gentle and harsh, kind and cruel. Quoting from Homer's *Hymn to Artemis*: *...She through the shadowy hills and the windy headlands rejoicing in the chase draws her golden bow, sending forth shafts of sorrow. Then tremble the crests of the lofty mountains, and terribly the dark woodland rings with din of beasts, and the earth shudders, and the teeming sea...* And Homer describes how, after the goddess of the hunt ends the chase, she *...goes to the great hall of her dear Phoebus Apollo, to the rich Delphian land; and arrays the lovely dance of Muses and Graces. There hangs she up her bended bow and her arrows, and all graciously clad about she leads the dances... while the others utter their immortal voice in hymns to fair-ankled Leto...Hail, ye children of Zeus and fair-tressed Leto...*

As I have already said, Artemis is a goddess of some importance, and can be soft, but also cruel.

An example of Artemis' cruelty is when she becalmed the entire Greek fleet at the beginning of the Trojan War. The reason being that King Agamemnon, on the occasion of the birth of his daughter Iphigenia, had vowed to sacrifice to the goddess the most beautiful possession he had. Since, however, his most beautiful possession was his new baby daughter, he'd failed to honour the vow.

The story is the plot of Euripides' tragedy *Iphigenia at Aulis*. In the drama King Agamemnon's seer warns the king that Artemis will not allow the fleet to sail till he has sacrificed Iphigenia, by then a teenage girl. When Iphigenia first learns of her fate, she is horrified. But gradually she realizes that it is her duty to give her life for the greater good of her people. The young girl refuses to be bound or held down, but proudly proffers her slender neck to the knife. But, miracle of miracles! As the priest is about to pierce the delicate skin, Artemis substitutes a hind in her place, and she is carried away by Artemis to become her priestess in Tauris (thought to be on the Crimean peninsula). With her sacrifice, the winds get up, and the fleet sets sail for Troy.

The story is picked up again in Euripides' *Iphigenia in Taurus*. In that drama Orestes, King Agamemnon's only son whose story is to be found in Aeschylus' trilogy the *Oresteia* (see Chapter 2), has been told by Apollo's oracle that if he is to rid himself of the few remaining Furies who still hound and harass him, he must retrieve and bring back to Greece a sacred image of Artemis which the king of Taurus holds in Artemis' temple there.

On his arrival at Taurus, Orestes together with his long-time friend Pylades, are compelled to hide their identity because, if it's discovered they are from Greece, then it is the law they must be killed.

However, when Iphigenia gradually discovers that Orestes is from her home city of Mycenae, she instantly wants to know what has happened to her family. Gradually she realizes that standing before her is none other than Orestes, her brother, last seen as a baby. What joy! Together they devise a plan to take the sacred image back to Greece, and the homesick Iphigenia decides to sail with them.

The rest of the drama is pure James Bond. It all might well have ended in disaster had it not been for the intervention of Athena. With her help the small party sails safely back to Brauron on the east coast of Greece. Where the boat comes ashore a temple of Artemis Brauronia was built in her honour, and the divine image was enshrined there. Legend has it that Iphigenia also was eventually entombed there.

Because the image of Artemis was so highly regarded at Brauron, a sanctuary of Artemis Brauronia was later erected also on the south-west corner of the Acropolis.

In Socrates' day he would have been keenly aware of the strange four-yearly ceremony in which young girls from good families, aged from eight to ten, walked from the Agora all the way to Brauron on the coast, dressed in animal skins. There they lived as wild animals for several years as attendants to the goddess at her sanctuary. The idea was, apparently, to get the wilder female nature out of the child. They were known as the 'Little Bears'. Then, at the age of twelve, the girls returned to their families, docile and ready for marriage. One wonders whether Socrates' spirited wife had been a 'Little Bear'; her shrewish character suggests she wasn't.

Artemis had two other temples of importance. The greatest was at Ephesus which at the time of Socrates was a colony of Greece. Her temple there was one of the seven wonders of the ancient world, and no doubt Socrates had heard of it. In the New Testament it is reported that St. Paul spent time in Ephesus, where there was a silversmith who made his living by creating and selling silver shrines of Artemis. When St. Paul preached there, those listening were outraged when he told them Artemis would soon be ...*deposed from her magnificence...(Acts 19:27)* Hackles rose and they shouted back: ..."*Great is Artemis of the*

Ephesians!"… (Acts 19:28)

John the Theologian was also said to have lived in Ephesus till he was banished by the Roman emperor, and fled to the Aegean island of Patmos – it was rumoured that he'd floated there on a cork. At the time Patmos had many pagan temples, but the most predominant was the one of Artemis which stood high above the port where the Monastery of John the Theologian now stands.

Interestingly, in the monastery museum there is an ancient marble plaque inscribed with words describing Patmos as *the loveliest island of the daughter of Leto which came up from the depth as a resting place of her* (Leto's) *wanderings*. Not only that but the same plaque also states that Orestes, son of King Agamemnon, had come there to Patmos, where he'd sacrificed to Artemis in thanks for being finally rescued from the torment of the Furies.

'The loveliest island of the daughter of Leto?' Oh, yes! The island is not only lovely but its grey-black volcanic rock exudes mystery. It is a jewel in the Aegean sea, wrought with creeks and coves, with the fortress monastery like a precious stone, a dark, gleaming pearl, dominating it.

While Harry and I were there, there was a full moon (appropriate, since Artemis was identified with the moon). On our first evening it was hidden behind a volcanic streak of cloud, and then slowly, slowly the cloud had thinned and the moon had reappeared. I told Harry that I thought it looked like an ancient fresco of the Day of Judgement, with the devils of black cloud being scattered as the light triumphed. Harry, who was less imaginative, said that it looked to him as if we were in for a spell of bad weather.

And so it proved to be. For several days we found ourselves marooned on the island – Patmos had no airport, and stormy weather meant no ferry-boats were sailing.

It was during this time that we met an earnest young Greek who had come to the island to get over the death of his mother. He asked us to join him in a drink and we had an interesting conversation. He brought up the subject of religion, and began speaking about the extraordinary phenomenon of consciousness. It was consciousness which made people feel there was an even greater consciousness, an all-embracing consciousness, which was God, he said.

I was at once a believer!

The consciousness of each individual was unique – everyone was unique, he said. No matter what nationality you were, no matter what happened to you in life (or when you died) you would never be anything other than the unique 'You'. That was an amazing thought! I had always been 'Me'? Yes, always, and would remain 'Me' throughout eternity, he said.

He spoke with such earnestness and conviction, it was as if the rest of the world ceased to exist as we sat by the quayside. Whilst making a point, he had a habit of raising his shoulders and bending both arms with clenched fists to his breast to give emphasis to his words.

Death? At death your soul was taken by St. Michael, he said. You were taken here and there and were shown the bad things and the good things you had done. Big panic! And, raising his shoulders and bending his arms with clenched fists to his breast again, he declared his conviction that a husband and wife were one body and, therefore, would be united in the next world. I'd glanced at Harry. Was he happy at the prospect of having me into life everlasting? Surely, one lifetime of me was quite enough for him? I was reassured by his smile, but suspected with such intense metaphysical stuff, he'd long ago stopped listening.

A few days later we were still marooned on the island.

It was the feast-day of Osios Christodoulos, the founder of the monastery, and we were invited by a monk to attend the Vigil held in his honour. Harry wasn't keen so I went alone. As usual, I was caught up in the beauty and atmosphere of the ancient Greek Orthodox Church: its candle-light from several silver, multiple-branched hanging candelabra and icon lamps, and its magnificent carved and gilded ornate *iconostasis* with its seventeenth century icons.

I was transported by the chanting and the incense – the Orthodox Church works on the five senses: sight, hearing, touch, smell and taste.

I was glad, however, that a taxi was coming to collect me at midnight. Just before I had to leave, it looked as if dawn was breaking as a light shone brightly through a small window high above the altar. It was the full moon. I then remembered that the monastery had been built on the site of the temple of Artemis, and the goddess was identified with the moon. Somehow all seemed significant that night.

But enough now of Artemis.

I would like to end this chapter with a visit I made to a temple of Apollo on Crete. It wasn't a major temple, but my visit to it made me experience the bleakness of being totally alone with nobody to turn to except – well, God! There! I, the God-doubter, have admitted it!

The incident occurred when Harry and I were at Gortyn, an archaeological site, and once an important Cretan city.

Harry had had enough of tramping around the excavations, and so I went alone to see Apollo's temple which was set apart in an olive grove about half a kilometre away.

St. Paul had once come to Gortyn, more by accident than intention, having been forced to seek shelter from a severe storm at sea. Apparently Titus, son of an illustrious pagan (some say a descendant of King Minos, no less) had been sent from Crete to Jerusalem to find out about this Christ whose new religion was being talked about. Whilst there, Titus had been baptized a Christian, and had arrived back on Crete with St. Paul who appointed him the first bishop of the island.

My fascination with the temple of Apollo, now only a few fallen columns in the heart of its olive-grove, was that in the second century A.D. it had been converted to a three-aisled Christian basilica; it had remained in use until the sixth century when a great cathedral dedicated to St. Titus was founded by the Emperor Justinian at Gortyn.

Standing by Apollo's temple I had wondered whether St. Paul had also stood there surveying the temple. Might he have foreseen it would be converted into a Christian church? The outline of the second century church was clearly visible – Christianity stamping itself on the pagan. It was very curious that St. Paul had become so one-eyed about the necessity to spread Christianity since he'd been born a Jew. For long he'd been a sworn enemy of all Christians until, wham! his sudden blinding light on the road to Damascus!

I was totally alone at this site and, when I left, I somehow missed the track along which I'd come. Instead, I walked deeper and deeper into the olive grove. I had no sense of direction, tried to take my bearings from the sun but headed west when I should have gone east (or the other way about). Anyone who has been lost in a forest of olive trees will know what a nightmare it can be.

I prayed to all the gods to get me out of this neverending olive grove. I was aware that maybe – yes, maybe! I was being taught a lesson for holding myself aloof from proper worship. Here I was, the great unbeliever, sort of saying sorry, and praying – more like imploring the Great Whatever.

I imagined God out there thinking to himself: 'There she goes again, crying out to me! I'll teach her a lesson this time. Let her learn humility! Didn't she stand before the holy relic of St. Titus' skull in Iraklion and show indifference instead of respect and reverence? Huh! Let her suffer! And did she not shrug and smile but turn away from my faithful nun who wanted her to buy a decorated elastic band of a bracelet, and even offered her a sweet in her kindness which she took and ate? Where was her charity? Where her compassion? Let her get lost!'

Consciousness – imagination – the fine line between standing aloof from deity, defying it even, then finding yourself alone and having to cope. One part of my conscious self told me that whether I believed or didn't, I would still have to do whatever I could by my own actions; another part was aware that outside assistance from an unseen power might make things easier and be a consolation because I wouldn't be so alone.

Not a soul to be seen, not a track to be found, only stony ground and olive trees – at least they offered spasmodic pools of shade. I decided to bypass God and appeal to Apollo. "Come on Apollo! Here's your chance! YOU get me out of here!"

I was finally rescued by an elderly Cretan peasant who I wouldn't let out of my sight till he'd led me to the path I needed and pointed out the way. And it wasn't till I at last found the main road that I was able to relax a little – was I even then heading in the right direction on the road? By that time I was so hot and addled, I wasn't sure of anything till I eventually rounded a bend and saw the main entrance to the Gortyn site. There I saw Harry shielding his eyes against the setting sun looking out for me. In answer to his explosive question, 'Where the hell have you been?' I gave the truthful answer, 'God alone knows!'

I never let on that on the road I'd passed a wayside shrine. I'd hesitated, then turned back to it. I'd felt a bit ridiculous, and conspicuous to passing motorists, as I stood before the shrine and sent up a prayer of thanks for my safe return, mumbling a sort of promise to mend my ways for ever after, yet knowing that I would almost certainly sink back to my lax old habits.

Enough of that! Enough too of Apollo, god of light, of music and of prophecy, and his twin sister Artemis. Socrates is waiting patiently in prison, and the sacred ship has just been spotted sailing round to the Saronic gulf on its return to Piraeus from Delos. The day of his execution is fast approaching. But a plan for his escape has been hatched up, and it is important to put it into action immediately.

CHAPTER 6

SOCRATES' LAST FEW DAYS OF LIFE
PLATO'S *CRITO*

The day of Socrates' execution is fast approaching, and he remains quietly confident that, having followed his 'inner voice', he is fulfilling his destiny.

When I first read a book about his trial and execution, I told Harry about Socrates' 'inner voice', to which he snorted "Your Soc sounds a bit mental to me!"

"But you surely believe in divine guidance?" I'd watched Harry across the kitchen table where we were having breakfast. As he bit into his toast and marmalade, I could see that the God-believer was having problems with the thought of divine guidance.

"I once had an 'inner voice'," I ventured. It was something I had never confessed to him before.

"You? An 'inner voice'?" Harry's expression was something between astonishment and alarm. It was as if I'd told him I'd seen a vision of the Virgin Mary. He chewed his toast in silence for a while. Eventually, he glanced at the kitchen clock, muttered, "Market day – bullocks!", scraped back his chair, took a gulp of his coffee half-standing, and added with a sly smile, "My 'inner voice' is calling!" And with that he was gone. The subject of my 'inner voice' was never mentioned again.

It is just before daybreak when Crito, a childhood friend of Socrates from his home village of Alopeke, arrives to visit him in prison. He is admitted by the prison warder who by now knows him as he's been a regular visitor over the past month.

Socrates immediately guesses that his friend is there at this early hour because the sacred boat has been spotted. Nevertheless, he asks why Crito has come so early. Crito explains that he's been there since before daybreak, but he didn't wake him earlier because he saw how peacefully he was sleeping. He adds how he's always admired Socrates' unflustered disposition, and his ability to face death so calmly and patiently.

To this Socrates replies that it would be ridiculous at his time of life to get over excited at the prospect of death.

The ship, though, hasn't yet docked at Piraeus, but has only rounded Sounion, the south-eastern point of Greece around which ships must sail from the Aegean sea to the Saronic gulf.

Socrates tells his friend that, thanks to being left to sleep on, he has just dreamt the boat will not be reaching Piraeus that day, and he believes he has another couple of days left before it docks.

Crito implores his friend to listen to a rescue plan he has for him. There's no time to lose, he says. He has enough money to bribe the guards, and enough also to support him and his family in exile. They must, though, take action that very night after dark.

But Socrates doesn't think it right to be rescued, and Crito becomes exasperated by his mulishness. He points out that if he allows Socrates to die he will lose an irreplaceable friend. It will also appear to many people that he could have saved him but had failed to do so, leaving his friends to think he wasn't prepared to waste money on trying to free him. What more shameful reputation could Socrates wish on him than that?

Socrates merely asks what does it matter what people think? To this Crito instantly replies that it matters a great deal; what people think is what has landed Socrates in gaol. Opinions matter, he insists, and if Socrates is worried that he, Crito and his friends, might have their property confiscated, and be made to pay hefty fines for rescuing him, then he can forget it, because they themselves feel justified in taking the risk. He pleads with Socrates, there's so little time left before his death, so he must listen attentively to what he's about to say. He has a plan and he must hear him out.

Knowing Socrates' stubborn streak, Crito tries to make him conscience-stricken. Socrates will, he says, bring upon himself his downfall which is exactly what his enemies want. Furthermore, Crito goes on, Socrates is letting down his three sons. He'll be deserting them, leaving them to fare as best they can without a father. He shouldn't have had children at all, if he wasn't prepared to see them through the difficult days of childhood and education. And he accuses Socrates of taking the easy way out.

The easiest way out? Death is Socrates' escape route? If Crito hopes to put pressure on Socrates by mentioning his responsibilities as a parent, he fails in this too. To Socrates the judgement has been passed according to Athenian law, and he must submit to the law of the land. It is the law that has built up Athens' reputation, and has brought her to be the great city she's become. He cannot be seen to be ducking the law while expecting everybody else to abide by it. No! He must do only what he knows is right: *My dear Crito, your zeal will be invaluable if it should have right on its side; but otherwise, the greater it is, the harder it makes matters…it is in my nature…to follow nothing within me but the principle which appears to me, upon reflection, to be best…If we cannot find better ones to maintain in the present situation, you can be sure that I won't agree with you – not even if the power of the populace threatens us, like children, with more bogeymen than it does now… (Crito 46b-c)*

It must not be forgotten that the oracle pronounced Socrates to be the wisest man in Greece. Nor must the two great maxims inscribed on the walls of Apollo's temple be belittled because they were pagan: 'Nothing in excess' and 'Know thyself'. Socrates firmly believed them to be two divine truths to be followed.

He continues to argue stubbornly, but good-naturedly with Crito, his would-be-saviour. Let them examine the matter together, he suggests, to see whether the principle can be seen differently. Should one disregard the principles of some human beings, while having a high regard for others? And, after a lot of preamble, he goes on to point out that you cannot suppose everyone's opinions to be right. For example, a man in training doesn't pay attention to praise or criticism from all and sundry, but listens carefully to the person training him.

Socrates finally makes the point that the important thing is not just to live, but to live honourably and justly. This leads to Socrates asking one final question: Will he and his rescuers be living justly if he chooses to be rescued, and so escape death? Or would he in truth be acting unjustly? In his judgement he would be acting unjustly.

So what are they all to do, Crito asks in desperation? And Socrates merely affirms what he's already said: *Then, even if one is unjustly treated, one should not return injustice, as most people believe – given that one should not act unjustly at all. (Crito 49b)*

He is almost Christ-like in submitting to the law, and appearing untroubled with death literally staring him in the face.

Socrates compares their situation with a child being scolded. A child was not on equal terms with his father or teacher giving him the right to answer back when scolded or strike back when beaten.

If, Socrates insists, a person chooses to live in Athens; if he's been born, brought up and has had a share in all her benefits, then it is, surely, unreasonable for that same individual to try to escape? Wise words! How often did I have to remind myself in those early dairy-farming days that I was sharing all the benefits Harry provided, and that it would be highly unreasonable of me to pack my bags and leave him to it! What did it matter if the smell of cow permeated my clothes and hair? Or that he sometimes interrupted my two sacred hours in the morning to summon me out for an urgent job that needed to be done! Stay with it and smile, woman! Go on and do your duty! Harry wasn't doing it for just himself but for me and the benefit of the family.

Socrates points out to Crito that he has spent all his life there in Athens and, therefore, has shown his contentment with the city under its laws, going daily to the Agora. Even more, he's fathered children and, during his defence, he could have proposed exile as an alternative penalty rather than death, but he didn't. And Socrates now, personifies the city's laws, and imagines them speaking to him should he flaunt them by escaping into exile. He says – or rather they, the Laws, say: ...*Yet now you...show no regard for us, the Laws, in your effort to destroy us. You are acting as the meanest slave would act, by trying to run away in spite of those compacts and agreements you made with us, whereby you agreed to be a citizen on our terms...you had seventy years in which it was open to you to leave if you were not happy with us... (Crito 49e)*

Can he, Socrates asks, possibly live happily if he sees his friend Crito and his co-conspirators helping him by subverting the law, and finding himself in exile with no rights and with no property? Under such circumstances, Socrates asks, would his life be worth living? And he ends with a final Socratic blast (the Athenian Laws are still speaking): *...Will no one observe that you, an old man with probably only a short time left to live, had the nerve to cling so greedily to life by violating the most important laws?...As for those principles of yours about justice and goodness in general — tell us, where will they be then?...is it for your children's sake that you wish to live, in order to bring them up and give them an education? How so? Will you bring them up and educate them by taking them off to Thessaly and making foreigners of them, so that they may gain that advantage too?...As things stand, you will leave this world (if you do) as one who has been treated unjustly not by us Laws, but by human beings... (Crito 53e-54e)*

And Socrates' final words to his friend are to let things rest as they are. It is his god who has brought him to this point.

So Socrates declines all offers of escape, believing it's his civil duty to accept the legal judgement of the court. He must, he says, remain in prison till his death.

But where exactly is this prison? Archaeologists, after comparatively recent excavations, believe it to be in the south-west corner of the Agora where a long rectangle of foundation stones mark it out. But there is another, more remote place I just happened to come across some years ago; there a prominent notice-board proclaimed it to be the 'Prison of Socrates'.

I was with two travelling companions and, late one June evening, the three of us took a stroll from our hotel along a path through a wooded area. Quite unexpectedly, we came on a clearing where before us were three cave-mouths in a rockface each one with prison bars. A notice-board proudly bore the words, 'Prison of Socrates'.

Knowing no better, we meekly accepted what the notice-board told us, and sat on a bench imagining Socrates spending his last days in that dark, dank triple cave.

How strange it is that humans have a Mind's Eye! That they can build a scenario of somebody who lived centuries in the past and visualize him imprisoned in a cave which he in all probability wasn't. How can the human mind get things so often wrong!

When I once pointed out this phenomenon to Harry, we happened to be cornering a bullock in a shed. "That's what it means to be human," he said. "But it's amazing!" I persisted. "To see what isn't before your eyes. Don't you think it extraordinary?" "Nothing strange about it – " The sentence got lost as he darted sideways with both arms out. "For God's sake, don't let it escape!" he shouted, and I waved a stout stick at the bullock.

A mere woman asserting herself over a bullock who, when all is said and done, is considerably stronger than her? Yet it cowered before me because it saw me with its two bovine eyes standing ferociously waving a stick. It struck me then that there seemed to be a natural hierarchy of things. The bullock saw me as all powerful (very sensibly with its eyes), whereas humans regard as all powerful an

Almighty God they do not see at all, using their Mind's Eye. Are animals to be admired for living their lives realistically, responding to their animal instincts? Are humans widely off the mark, thanks to their Mind's Eye?

From Socrates' gaol we continued on along the footpath till we came to a wide open space with extensive views. Here the ground was hard-packed and stony. There was a raised area and with excitement I read a notice saying we were on the Pnyx. Here was where democracy had been born, where orators had addressed assembled Athenian citizens who'd then cast their votes for or against the proposals put to them. Close by were the remains of a sanctuary of Zeus which added solemnity to the site.

It was here that Pericles had swayed the masses with his oratory, and whose vision had turned Athens into a rich and powerful city-state; here too that later politicians had faltered and brought Athens to her knees.

From where we stood that evening on the Pnyx, as the sun went down and the amber sky grew darker, we could see the distant, sombre cone-like outline of Mount Lykabettos in the north-east which, according to legend, the goddess Athena had accidentally dropped while carrying it to buttress her Acropolis. Nearer was the Areópagus where murder trials had been held, and where Orestes had been acquitted of his matricide. To the south was the Hill of the Muses with its long evening shadows and the great marble monument of Philopappos (third century A.D.) rearing up through the trees. And to the east was the Acropolis with the dark silhouette of the Parthenon. Just north of the Areópagus was the Agora where Socrates had spent so many of his waking hours. And north-west, crowning the Kolones Agoraios hill (but not in view) was the important temple of Hephaestus, god of fire and metal-work. Built by

Ictinus, the same architect responsible for the Parthenon, the Hephaisteion is said to be the best preserved temple left in Greece with its exterior and interior of many marble columns, and a wood and marble coffered ceiling. Its sculpted marble frieze and metopes portray the usual Battle of the Lapiths and Centaurs, and also the Labours of Theseus and the Labours of Heracles.

How apt that the Agora, that remarkable area of civic and everyday working life, should have watching over it from the south-east, the Parthenon atop the Acropolis, temple of Athena, goddess of arts and craft and weaving; and from the north-west the Hephaisteion, temple of Hephaistus, god of fire and metal-work.

When St. Paul came to Athens he, surely, would have been impressed by the numerous temples. He must have noticed the marble wonders that remained of Pericles' Athens – admittedly, many damaged by war but, nevertheless, still prominently visible. He could not have been blind to the Hephaisteion or the Parthenon, though he never mentioned them, despite spending some time in Athens whilst awaiting his two companions Silas and Timothy.

As reported in the Acts of the Apostles: ...*his spirit was provoked within him as he saw that the city was full of idols. So he argued...in the market place* (Agora) *every day with those who chanced to be there. Some also of the...philosophers met him. And some said, "What would this babbler say?" Others said, "He seems to be a preacher of foreign divinities"* – because *he preached Jesus and the Resurrection... (Acts 17:17-18)*

His visit was, of course, over four centuries after Socrates himself had argued every day in the 'market place'. The only thing St. Paul mentioned was an altar he had come across with an inscription 'To an unknown god'.

That he seized on and, by sleight of hand, or rather sleight of words, said: *What therefore you worship as unknown, this I proclaim to you. The God who made the world and everything in it, being Lord of heaven and earth, does not live in shrines made by man, nor is he served by human hands, as though he needed anything, since he himself gives to all men life and breath and everything… (Acts 17:23-25)*

In fact, the altar to an unknown god that St. Paul commented on was there for anyone grateful for some benefit received, but who didn't know which god to thank.

What, we might wonder, would Socrates have thought of St. Paul had they met – or St. Paul of Socrates, for that matter? No doubt, Socrates would immediately have questioned the apostle on what he meant by God and Resurrection? Did St. Paul have the Knowledge, Socrates would have wanted to know, or only Belief? Define Knowledge. Define Belief. And they would have sparred verbally until time ran out, which it never fails to do. Each would then have gone his own way – St. Paul still with his Belief in the Resurrection of Christ, and Socrates with the Knowledge that he did not know. The early Greeks were religious, but the word Faith was unknown. Piety towards their gods was the nearest thing.

Here we must now leave Socrates to his last few days of life, since Crito has failed in his attempt to rescue him. In which prison, though, remains uncertain.

CHAPTER 7

POSEIDON, GOD OF THE SEA

When I described the marbles on the Parthenon in Chapter 1, I never mentioned those on the west pediment which portrayed Poseidon and Athena competing for the patronage of the city. Apparently, in deepest antiquity, a contest was set between them and, whoever presented the city with the most useful gift was promised the patronage of the city. Poseidon immediately struck the acropolis with his trident, and up gushed a completely useless spring of salt water – perhaps he didn't want the patronage. Athena, on the other hand, presented them with an olive tree, a most helpful gift as it gave food, olive oil, fuel for lamps, wood for building, leaves for wreath-making, and so on. So Athena was proclaimed the winner which explains why the city was named after her. Much later, perhaps to compensate Poseidon, a very fine temple was built and dedicated to him at Sounion.

Cape Sounion is the most south-easterly point on mainland Greece. The great fifth century B.C. temple with its many remaining marble columns still dominates the headland; the columns draw the eye to where they rise white and majestic above the flat-topped promontory; they are a major landmark for mariners who sail down the Aegean and round to the Saronic Gulf – the pure white marble used for its construction was quarried from nearby.

There at Sounion the goddess Athena also has a temple but much less prominently placed on a lower level inland. There she gives her uncle Poseidon supremacy as god of the sea, which is only right.

Yes, the temple on its headland is impressive, even though shorn of its sculpted frieze depicting the usual Battle of the Centaurs and Lapiths and the Battle of the Gods and Giants, chunks of which can be seen in museums around Europe.

It was springtime when Harry and I first visited Sounion and, to quote straight from my notebook at the time: '…all around the promontory are wild flowers, white and pink clumps of cistus, scarlet poppies, pale mauve stock, wild iris, grape hyacinth and bright yellow gorse. We've just walked along the cliff-top and surveyed the rocky coastline. From here we can see the island of Aegina to the south-west, the southern tip of the long island of Euboea to the north, the Hymettos mountains to the west, and even maybe the faint outline of Asia Minor to the east. The sea below is a superb dark inky blue except around the rocks where it is an amazing turquoise.'

It would have been easy there to imagine (had I thought about it, but at that time I was a novice on the mythology of Greece) that Poseidon, though an Olympian god, lived with his wife Amphitrite, daughter of the sea-god Nereus, in a gold palace in the depth of the sea.

★

Poseidon was described by Homer as quick-tempered; his ability to whip up the sea and throw violent storms caused mariners to respect and fear him.

Socrates, brought up on Homer's *Odyssey*, would have known how Odysseus became the victim of Poseidon's rage. This was because Odysseus had blinded Polyphemus, Poseidon's one-eyed Cyclops son. As a result Poseidon threw violent storms at him, caused shipwreck, sent sea monsters, and enticed him with enchantresses, so delaying his homeward journey by ten years – stories of the sort schoolboys love.

Odysseus could hardly be blamed for blinding Polyphemus since he and his companions had been taken prisoner by him and held captive in his cave. He'd already proved to be a savage having seized two of Odysseus' companions and banged their heads on the cave's rock-floor as though they were new-born puppies so their *brains spurted out*. Polyphemus then tore them apart and devoured them till *entrails and flesh, marrow-bones and all were consumed*.

How the schoolboy Socrates would have loved the description of Odysseus' escape from Polyphemus' cave! He would have read avidly about how Odysseus had given his savage captor a bowlful of excellent vintage wine which so pleased him, that he gulped down great quantities of it till he toppled to the floor and fell asleep. Then the wine containing morsels of human flesh was vomited up from Polyphemus' throat.

What more gruesome details could a schoolboy ask for! The child Socrates would have revelled in how the cunning Odysseus gouged out the one eye of Poseidon's son with a red-hot pointed olive-wood stake so that the blood sizzled ...*and the roots of his eye crackled in the heat*.

And escape Odysseus did, only to be faced with endless maritime adventures one after another, each one of which would have inspired the young Socrates.

★

Poseidon was not just god of the sea, but was also god of earthquakes for which he was known as 'the earth-shaker'.

It was Poseidon's divine displeasure which had once brought an end to the inhabitants of ancient Santorini, if the following story is to be believed. It is supposed by many to be the lost island of Atlantis whose disappearance was caused by a violent subterranean eruption.

In Plato's *Critias* Socrates listens in silence (it's not often he stays silent) while Critias describes the following ancient story which he's heard from a reliable source. At the beginning of time the gods had divided up the world equally amongst themselves, and Poseidon had received the sea together with the island of Atlantis. Poseidon subsequently gave equal portions of Atlantis to his five sets of twin sons born of a mortal woman. Each ruled his share with great success, meaning that everyone became wealthy, generous and content. But, as in all extended times of prosperity and contentment, life got monotonous, and the descendants of these sons became increasingly disgruntled, even aggressive. Eventually, Poseidon could bear them no longer, so with a flick of the hand he caused a great earthquake. The result was that the weight of the island (originally round) collapsed in on itself causing a huge tsunami; it is this tsunami, so it is thought, that destroyed the Minoan civilization on Crete one hundred and seventeen miles south – over a nine hours' sail away.

But oh, how beautiful the island of Santorini is today! Anyone visiting Fira, the main town perched at the top of great volcanic cliffs, can look across what is known as the caldera (where the centre of the island sank) to the dark, volcanic islands beyond, which were once a part of Santorini.

The scenery from Fira is spectacular: a huddle of white-washed cubic houses built higgledy-piggledy down the charcoal-grey volcanic rockface with the occasional rounded blue dome of a church, to the small port and glittering sapphire-blue sea seven hundred steps down.

Strings of mules with colourful trappings and tinkling bells bearing their burdens (mostly tourists) accompanied by their rugged muleteers, zig-zag up and down a flag-stoned track to and from the port where yachts and white cruise-liners lie at anchor.

On our last evening there, Harry was hoping to sit peacefully on our terrace, eating scraps of left-overs from our fridge while we watched the sunset. I tried to accept this frugal plan, but the thought of not riding a mule dogged me. I must have behaved like an impossible child till he could stand me no longer – where was the peace he'd been hoping for? In exasperation he gave in and we had the mule ride, catching the mule-train on its final ascent in the glow of the evening sunset which turned the white cubic houses a glowing pink, and the sea on fire. The quiet rhythmic motion of my mule as it carried me up the shallow steps, sure-footed and docile filled me with joy. When we reached the top of the town, the sun appeared to be poised above the horizon, casting a sheen along the silver-grey caldera; the eye of my mule glinted as it reflected the light.

Eventually, the flight of shallow steps ended, and we approached an alleyway which led out to open country.

We dismounted, and I thanked my muleteer, and thanked my mule whose name was Christos, and spoke words of endearment into its long ear, and stroked its furry forehead. Christos remained quite indifferent, but I was overjoyed with my ride. The string of mules then continued on their way with their tinkling bells and the muffled sound of their numerous hooves.

"That cost ten euros!" Harry grumbled.

But the expense didn't end there. I was completely parched from the excitement, and a little refreshment was needed. Harry must have felt the same because we entered an inviting looking taverna which had small round mosaic-topped tables and alabaster lamps. From there we had a view down to the caldera far below, where the sun by now had dipped below the horizon, leaving the sea a gleaming pewter, and the islands black silhouettes against an amber sky.

It wasn't a place to ask for only a glass of water. To my surprise, Harry was all smiles and said he'd like a glass of wine.

Greek music rose romantically from one of the numerous tavernas on a lower terrace.

"Much better than eating scraps from our fridge!" I said. "Let's have a grand finale meal here – well, a small finale." I didn't want to overdo it.

Bravely I said to our charming waitress – at the time we were the only couple there – that we hadn't planned to eat out but it was so pleasant, could we have the smallest something, please.

And oh, how memorable that small something was! A basket of warm, crusty bread, a small container of a soft buttery mixture with a dash of cinnamon, a small bowl of tzatziki (yoghurt, cucumber and garlic), accompanied by a plate of haloumi (flat, round goat's cheese) cut into neat triangular pieces, lightly fried and sprinkled with lemon juice squeezed over it with a flourish of the waitress' hand.

By the time we'd devoured every morsel of everything, other couples had arrived looking elegant in dresses and suits, putting us to shame in our mule-riding clothes.

When the bill was brought, it was discreetly concealed in a folded leather case. Harry grabbed it from me and put on his spectacles. He read it from every angle and eventually hissed: "Seventy euros! That's monstrous! Ten euros a glass of wine!!" By then we'd had several glasses. "Damn your mule ride!"

"Damn your scraps from the fridge!" I said. I felt elated by the whole evening's wild extravagance. "It's something we'll never forget, and been worth every penny!"

So ended our memorable stay on Santorini.

There were other areas of Greece which were held sacred to Poseidon. In north-east Greece, the whole landmass of Chalkidiki was shaped like his three-pronged trident as though he'd once laid claim to the area. The third prong was Mt. Athos, the Holy Mountain, also known as 'The Garden of the Mother of God'. In antiquity it was believed to have been the mountain of the gods before Mt. Olympus became their accepted domain. Legend has it that, during some almighty family quarrel amongst the Olympian gods, a son of Poseidon hurled a mountain from the mainland at his father and there for ever afterwards it had remained embedded. To stop this unholy quarrel the territory was made over to Poseidon. Afterwards, however, there were such rumblings of anger and displeasure from

Zeus, that the mountain was finally offered back to him. Thoroughly affronted, Poseidon expressed his fury by whipping up frequent and sudden storms of such severity, that mariners have been wary of sailing around that headland ever since.

Today, the Holy Mountain is isolated from the hurly-burly excesses of modern day life, and is an autonomous Orthodox monastic centre where women are totally forbidden. This is due to the arrival there of the Virgin Mary in 54 A.D. Apparently, when the Virgin stepped ashore, all the shrines and temples of the Olympian gods (and there were many), crashed to the ground, and the voices of the gods confessed aloud that they were false. The Virgin Mary immediately declared Mt. Athos to be hers, and no other woman was allowed to set foot on it. This has been the case ever since, and even female cats are evicted.

When staying at Ouranopoulos, the small town at the head of the Holy Mountain (the name means 'Heavenly City'), Harry and I one evening followed a well-marked track – about a two mile walk – to the Athos Gate. There, huge notice-boards warned of police prosecution if anyone was found trespassing on the hallowed territory beyond the locked, metal gate set in its high wire-mesh fence. A bleak looking grey stone building with the Greek flag flying from a flag-pole was, I suspected the police look-out. Beyond the wire fence was a forest of trees, bottle-green, shadowy and sombre in the evening light. I was surprised to see a wide triangular piece of the wire fence cut away, so allowing anyone to hop in or out – a tempting gap, but perhaps the police had their field glasses trained on it.

I persuaded Harry to follow me along the wire-mesh fencing down to the sea. There we sat on a couple of boulders on the sea-shore right there beside the Holy

Mountain. It was as close as I was ever likly to get to the forbidden territory. All boats were required by law to be five hundred metres off-shore at the very least. The Eve in me was sorely tempted to swim along and set foot on the Holy Mountain itself, or to rise like Aphrodite from the waves to view the inhabitants. But due to my respect for the powers that be, either divine or human, or because Harry would most certainly have hauled me back, or maybe because I'm no swimmer and would more likely have drowned in the attempt, I remained seated where I was, content just to be there: to watch the sea take on a metallic hue, before turning a fiery red as the sun began to set.

It was on the coast at the neck of the first Chalkidiki prong (named Kassandra), that Socrates had fought as a soldier alongside Alcibiades at Potidaea. The name Potidaea was given it by the Corinthians who took over the town in the seventh century B.C. giving it the Doric version of their name for Poseidon. In the fifth century B.C. a rebellion broke out in the town due to Pericles' annual tribute to be paid to Athens by members of the Delian League of which Potidaea was a member. The rebellion had to be subdued so the army was called in. Socrates was called up and served as a hoplite (a heavily armed foot soldier), as was Alcibiades (of Plato's *Symposium* fame in which he declared his love for Socrates). As a wealthy aristocrat, however, Alcibiades was in the cavalry.

On Socrates' return to Athens (thought to be in the summer of 429 B.C.), he went straight back to his habitual haunts, on this occasion to the Taureas' wrestling ground where he was immediately recognized. In Plato's dialogue

Charmides he describes how Chaerephon (the same man who enquired of the oracle who was the wisest), on spotting Socrates entering, immediately leapt up from where he was seated with a group of friends; he wanted to know about the news they'd just heard of a bloody battle that had been fought a few days earlier in which many Greeks had died. Chaerephon asks whether Socrates was involved, and is amazed to hear he was. Socrates takes the horrors of battle in his stride as he does with any hardship he has to face.

At the wrestling ground he is introduced to a handsome young man whose body is unusually fine: Socrates is always drawn to such adolescents, but especially if he is told the young man is a poet and a budding intellectual.

Socrates immediately gets a dialogue going with the young man, the subject being Knowledge, Self-control and whether one knows what one knows. I am introducing Plato's *Charmides* here to demonstrate how Socrates sets about testing the young man's intelligence – which means the intelligence of any reader, me included. He must have had the ability to charm and hold the attention of his audience while he examines at length and in detail, the exact meaning of what is meant by Knowledge. To me I can put it in one sentence: Knowledge is to know. By the end of a long, and what I thought an incredibly unnecessary probe into the meaning of the word, Socrates finally remarks that he can see Critias (the cousin of the young and handsome Charmides) is in *the snares of perplexity*.

Maybe there was some vital point in Socrates' argument I'd missed, but I wasn't surprised Critias was in the *snares of perplexity*. I only knew – and I knew that I knew, however hard one tried to define the word Knowledge – that Socrates could at times be incredibly irritating!

★

Another major site where Poseidon was greatly honoured was down south in the Peloponnese. Apart from compulsory military service for every Athenian citizen between the age of eighteen and thirty – and in times of war he might well be called up if under the age of sixty – the only occasion Socrates was known to have voluntarily left Athens, was to attend the Isthmian Games. These were held every second year in the spring at Isthmia on the isthmus just east of Corinth.

Poseidon was not only god of the sea and earthquakes but god of horses also. There at the Isthmian Games he was, no doubt, invoked by all who competed in the horse- and chariot-races. Other contests consisted of athletics, boxing, wrestling, and included events also for musicians and poets. A winner at the Isthmian Games was held in the highest esteem, and all competitors regarded the Games as a preparation for the even more prestigious Olympics.

The second century A.D. travel-writer Pausanias described Poseidon's Isthmian sanctuary as he had seen it – a far cry from today's tumbled ruins: *As you go into the sanctuary, there are portrait statues of athletes who won at the Isthmian Games, and some pine trees in a line, mostly growing straight up. The temple itself is no higher than the trees; there are bronze Tritons standing on it. In the front of the temple there are two Poseidons, and Amphitrite* (Poseidon's wife) *and a Sea, all bronze...* This, surely, would have been as Socrates would have seen it.

The winner of each contest was crowned with a wreath of wild celery, an award which didn't go unnoticed by St. Paul who, in his effort to reach out to the pagan mind, asked why an athlete would want to go to all the trouble of disciplining the body, when only one competitor could be the victor, and a *perishable wreath* was all he could expect as an award. Much better for him to discipline himself for Christ, as he would then gain a wreath which was *imperishable*. Oh, how sanctimonious St. Paul was! Was he not able to enjoy the Games and soak up the atmosphere? Could he never enter into the spirit of a pagan event?

The sanctuary is situated high above the sea and still holds a certain mystique, even though it is a jumble of fallen column-drums and ruined foundation stones. Only the Roman baths contain an undamaged and exquisite floor-mosaic depicting Nereids, octopuses and fish in a swift flowing movement, very much in keeping with Poseidon and the sea. From there you are able to look down over the Saronic Gulf.

Far below in the horseshoe bay fringed by low mountains, was where St. Paul arrived at the ancient port of Kenchreai having set sail from Athens, and from there that he'd then sailed on to Ephesus. The remains of the ancient quays and warehouses of ancient Kenchreai are still visible where they lie submerged in the clear shallow waters along the shore. A partly turfed-over, stone-slabbed pathway (the ancient Sacred Way) still exists, along which competitors and spectators once walked from the port to the sanctuary for the Games.

Apparently, the port of Kenchreai was named after Kenchrias, a son of Poseidon, as was Lechaion (Corinth's western port) named after another son Lechis. The mother of these two sons was Peirene, a nymph and daughter of a river-god. When Kenchrias was accidently killed, Peirene was inconsolable and wept so copiously and unceasingly, it is said she turned into a spring – Peirene's spring, where her tears continue to flow to this day; it can still be seen at the archaeological site at Corinth.

But never mind all that! And never mind St. Paul's one-eyed antipathy to all pagan celebrations! I will end this chapter with another quite unbelieveable but wonderful piece from the *Iliad* which Homer sang about Poseidon in the Trojan War who, when he saw the Greeks being pushed back to the sea and their ships being torched, came to their assistance. He strode down from a mountain peak where he'd been watching their perilous situation, and the *...high hills and forests shook under the immortal feet of the descending god. He took three strides and with the fourth reached Aegae, his goal, where his impressive palace built of gleaming gold stands under the depths of the waters...There he harnessed to his chariot his two bronze-hooved horses, with their flowing golden manes. He clothed himself in gold, seized his well-wrought lash of gold, mounted his chariot and drove out across the waves. The sea beasts frolicked beneath him, on all sides out of the deep, for well they knew their lord. The sea itself stood back for him, so that his bounding horses bore him on, and the bronze axle of his chariot remained dry below as they carried him towards the Achaean fleet... (Iliad Bk. 13: 18-32)*

There we must leave Poseidon because the sacred ship has at last docked at Piraeus, and the execution of Socrates can no longer be delayed.

CHAPTER 8

SOCRATES' DEATH
PLATO'S *PHAEDO*

The sacred ship is back, the annual mission to Delos is completed, and there is nothing now to delay the execution of Socrates. Knowing this must be his last morning of life, many close friends and philosophers have arrived early at the prison to visit him. They are, however, asked by the porter to wait because Socrates has with him his wife Xanthippe and one of his sons.

Having heard that well-wishers and fellow philosophers have come to see him, there is nothing Socrates would like more than to engage with them on some interesting discussion – he is not one for emotional and painful farewells, and the porter is soon back to invite them all in.

When they enter, Xanthippe remarks bluntly that this will be her husband's last opportunity to debate some topic. Socrates asks one of his friends to accompany his wife and son back home – their tears of distress can be heard as the two depart, yet Socrates remains calm.

We know that Xanthippe has a reputation for being a shrew of a wife and always complaining, and that Socrates was a very trying husband. His former student Xenophon, however, describes how Socrates once stood up for his wife, and strongly reprimanded his eldest son Lamprocles when he was rude to her: *'Look here, my boy, you know that there are some people who are called ungrateful?…Are you clear about what it is that people do to earn this name?'* And in a convoluted way (which, no doubt, his son was never to forget), he drew attention to all that his mother had done for him unstintingly since the day he was born. According to Xenophon, the conversation went as follows:

'Which kind of ferocity do you think is harder to bear – a wild beast's or a mother's?'

'A mother's,' he said, *'if she's like mine.'*

'Has she ever injured you by biting or kicking, as a good many people have suffered before now from wild animals?'

'Oh, no,' he said, *'but she says things that one wouldn't want to hear every day of one's life.'*…

At least the son sounds spirited, though Socrates gradually wears him down: *'So if you are sensible, my boy, you will beseech the gods to pardon any disregard that you have shown towards your mother in case they count you as ungrateful and refuse to do you good; and at the same time you will take care that your fellow men don't observe you neglecting your parents and all lose respect for you so that you stand revealed as destitute of friends…'* (Xen. Memoirs: 2.2.1-2.2.9)

But we are now in Socrates' last hours. The prison warder has just removed a fetter from his leg, and he is sitting up in bed flexing it. After a moment he announces how extraordinary it is that from the pain of being fettered comes the pleasure of having it removed. He rubs his leg which is sore, and comments on how odd the word 'pleasant' is in relation to its opposite which is 'painful'. How curious that the two cannot affect a person at the same time.

The execution will not take place till after sunset that day and it is still early morning. What a torment those few remaining hours would be for most people awaiting execution.

Unlike Socrates who faces death head-on with intense interest, when I am confronted by the mortality of family or friends, I refuse to look death in the eye. The word 'death' is taboo as I put on my all-must-stay-alive armour. I am certain that if Harry or I were terminally ill, we wouldn't cling to each other weeping, or discuss the taboo subject, but would talk amusing banalities and find things from the past to laugh about till whichever of us was dying lost consciousness.

Not facing death fair and square as Socrates did, I suspect – I know – is a self-defence mechanism. It is where Apollo's maxim stands me in good stead: 'Know thyself'. Knowing myself, I am only too aware that, once emotion gets a grip of me, I become a quivering wreck, sucked down into my whirlpool of misery. Best to keep it at arm's length.

Give me Socrates who is unemotional, and is deeply interested in what death entails. He treats death as if he is about to travel off abroad on holiday; he is looking forward to what new interesting surprises lie in store for him.

Socrates tells his friends how he has been filling the time by turning Aesop's fables into verse. Aesop! What better way for Socrates to amuse himself alone in prison with death looming, than to play about with the sixth century B.C. Aesop's moral tales.

The 'North Wind and the Sun' is just one example out of over three hundred and fifty, and Socrates, so it is said, knew them all by heart. The story is as follows: The North Wind challenges the Sun to a contest in strength by seeing which of them can get a coat off a traveller the quickest.

The North Wind is confident he can, and blows with great force; the traveller, however, only feels the cold, and the harder the North Wind blows, the more clothes the man puts on. The Sun, in contrast, shines gently to begin with, and in no time the man takes off his coat. The Sun gradually grows hotter and hotter till the man strips off and dives into the nearest river. So the Sun wins. The moral to the tale being that gentle persuasion is more effective than brute force – something Socrates would have appreciated.

Being a man charged with curiosity, Socrates launches into a long discussion about the immortality of the soul, and how it is through the soul that men come to be aware of God and the eternal. He speaks of the soul's repeated recycling of itself. Death, he suggests, is nothing but the separation of the soul from the body. What else can it be, he asks?

Oddly enough, I have always thought it significant when, on the day my mother died in hospital, I heard a new-born baby's cry. It occurred to me then that her soul on death had been released and drawn back into the new-born child with its first breath. Fanciful? Maybe.

Socrates goes on to say that, while in the company of the body, the soul is quite unable to remain pure because of the body's countless distractions – its lusts, fantasies, needs, desires and any amount of rubbish, as he puts it. It is the body which prevents us from thinking pure thoughts, he insists.

Since he himself has cast off the enjoyments and comforts of everyday life for the sake of his soul – remembering he possesses only one cloak and goes about barefoot – he points out how unreasonable it would be for him now to fear death, having prepared himself for it all his life. And, after a great deal of discussion about the soul's dilemma at being imprisoned in a living body, and the temperance needed to pacify it, he suggests philosophy (the love of wisdom) is nothing less than a purifying rite.

Socrates then goes on to speak of those who first established initiation rites: of Demeter's Eleusian Mysteries (see Chapter 2), and Orpheus' mystic religion known as Orphism. They both, he says, give whoever is initiated and purified the belief that they will have eternal life, ... *For truly there are, so say those concerned with the initiations, "many who bear the wand, but few who are devotees"...'* – the wand-bearers being the Maenads, followers of Dionysos – how similar this sounds to Jesus saying in a parable ...*'For many are called, but few are chosen.' (Matthew 22:14)* referring to the kingdom of heaven.

Orpheus, is generally thought to be the son of Apollo and the Muse Calliope whose own mother was Mnemosyne (the name means 'memory' – and where would humans be without memory!)

Orpheus was a man of peace, of poetry and gentleness. He was renowned for his singing which, it is said, was so sublime that the mountains bowed down to hear him, and fish leapt from the sea in wonder.

Today Orpheus is mainly remembered for the loss of his beloved Eurydice who, as his young bride, died from a venomous snake bite. Orpheus was so distraught that the immortals were sorry for him and allowed him to fetch Eurydice back from Hades. Taking his lyre with him, Orpheus charmed Charon the ferryman with his singing as he was rowed across the river Styx, and had Cerberus, the fierce three-headed guard-dog, fawning with pleasure at the gates of Hades. When he reached the presence of Lord Hades and Persephone in their subterranean kingdom, they gave him permission to take Eurydice back to the land of the living on the one condition he didn't look back at her on his way up.

Overjoyed, he led Eurydice up through the labyrinth of the underworld but (as I've already described in the *Symposium* chapter), as they approached the light, Orpheus glanced back to make sure she was still following, and that was that. His beautiful young bride vanished for good, never to be seen again. Such finality!

Totally overwrought, Orpheus from then on shunned the company of all women. This greatly angered Dionysos' women Maenads who turned on him and in one of their frenetic ecstasies, tore him limb from limb, and threw his head into one of the rivers on Mt. Olympus. One legend has it that the Maenads then washed their blood-stained hands in the river but, horrified, it vanished underground, and didn't resurface till it reached the sacred site of Dion four miles or so away. Another legend was that Orpheus' head, still singing, together with his lyre, floated down river to the Aegean sea and was eventually washed up on the island of Lesbos where it ended up in a cave. From there it is said it delivered oracles to the locals, till Apollo put an end to it, declaring that oracle pronouncements were his exclusive province.

Harry and I once visited Lesbos with the express purpose of seeing the river up which Orpheus' head had floated, and the cave where it had ended up. We were accompanied by the Stoic – the woman who had travelled around Cyprus hunting down Aphrodite's haunts, as she liked the idea of another trip chasing legends with us.

"All the way here, I ask you, to find some wretched cave!" said Harry scathingly, hoping to get the Stoic's backing so we could all go to the sea for a swim.

"His head still singing and attached to his lyre which

was still playing," I added.

"And why not? This is the island of poetry, music and imagination," said the Stoic soothingly.

"And the cave we were looking for just now, where they were blasting the mountainside – the cave we couldn't see, and which probably doesn't exist – was apparently the fellow's oracle," Harry scoffed.

The quarried mountainside we'd passed (no cave visible) had been of a rather beautiful salmon pink rock. I'd asked about it at an isolated taverna – at least they knew the legend and took my interest seriously. Yes, archaeologists had been up there but had found nothing, I was informed. Yes, we could get up to it but it was inadvisable in this midday heat, and yes, there was absolutely nothing to see (this to Harry) once you were there.

With detailed instructions how to get to the spot where Orpheus' head had floated up river, we set off again, and almost at once were driving alongside a river whose banks were lush with tall reeds and, amazingly, had water flowing in it – nearly every other one we'd seen had been a dry river-bed.

Eventually we'd arrived at Ancient Antissa, the so-called estuary near an isolated promontory where the head had floated in.

"I like it," said the Stoic, sitting on a low stone wall. "There's a certain mystique to the place, a *je ne sais quoi*, if you know what I mean."

I stared out at the calm, glittering sheen of the Aegean sea, and tried to imagine a singing head, together with a lyre, bobbing along to the island. But the vision grated with the charm and beauty of the place.

"Well, now we're here let's enjoy what there is," said the Stoic tactfully. "So what else did your Orpheus do apart from fetching Eurydice back from Hades, and his head floating all the way here?"

"He left sacred writings – but only scraps of them remain," I said, disappointed at my inability to say much more.

"And?"

"He believed in the purity of the soul and the impurity of man, and taught that each life was an opportunity, through right-living, to bring the soul closer to the divine – rather Christian, don't you think?"

"Nothing Christian about it," said Harry firmly. "Just more fanciful nonsense!"

"As is the case with so many religions," said the Stoic placidly. "We have to admire the extraordinary imaginations of those early minds able to conjure up such fanciful stories."

Fortunately on Lesbos, there had been worthwhile sites which both Harry and the Stoic had enjoyed, so the journey hadn't been a total damp squib – bird-watching on salt marshes was one of them, and the Taxiarchis Monastery which possessed a miracle working icon of the Archangel Michael was another. The Archangel was said to have taken over from the Roman god Mercury, who'd taken over from Hermes in conducting the souls of the dead to the next world. The difference being that Christian archangels had large wings, while Mercury and Hermes had only tiny ones, and not on their shoulders but on their feet and their broad-brimmed hats. 'Very inferior!' was Harry's comment.

Orpheus' head, I supposed, had been a resurrection of a sort – a death that hadn't quite happened since his head continued singing and some of his mystical teachings had survived. Certainly Dionysos was said to die annually and to rise again at Delphi, as did Persephone at Eleusis also.

Astonishingly, there exists today a third century A.D. image of a crucified body nailed to a cross which, at first sight, could be taken to be an image of the crucified Christ. Below the cross, however, are two words inscribed in Greek: 'Orpheus – Bakkikoc'. 'Bakkikoc' is a variant of Bacchus, the Roman name for Dionysos. Depictions of the crucified Christ hanging on the cross did not begin till the fourth century. But maybe the third century A.D. image of the crucified Orpheus was a Christian way intended to show the death of Orphism?

Of even greater interest to me is the fact that, after the conquest of Palestine by Alexander the Great in the fourth century B.C., there had been an attempt to Hellenize the Jews.

At the time of Christ there had been many Gentiles in Galilee who worshipped the Greek gods and, no doubt, many were devotees of Dionysos (or Bacchus as he was known by the Romans). According to the evangelist John (a Galilean fisherman) in the Gospel of John, Jesus said: "I am the true vine." True vine! Why did he say that? Was he implying that there was no truth in Dionysos with his bunches of grapes? And in the same Gospel, Jesus said also: "I am the bread of life". Why use those words? Was he here negating the divinity of Demeter, goddess of corn?

Back to Socrates in his last hours pondering aloud whether he has achieved the purity of soul he has always striven for or not.

He is endlessly patient and kindly disposed with Simmias and Cebes (two young Pythagorean philosophers) who are involved in his discussion on the soul. In a short interlude, they are seen talking quietly between themselves. Eventually they admit that they fear upsetting Socrates at this critical moment when death is looming. But Socrates merely chuckles and wants to know what's troubling them.

Cebes boldly asks whether on death it isn't just as likely that the soul disappears like breath or a puff of smoke. Is Socrates able to convince him that the soul continues and possesses power and energy?

Socrates answers kindly, and a long discussion follows on the subject of the soul being recycled. Socrates' logic is that opposites come into being only from their opposites, such as Beauty from Ugliness, Justice from Injustice and so on. What, therefore, is the opposite to dying? Clearly it is coming to life again, just as sleeping is to re-awakening.

He then goes on to say: *'In that way… we're agreed that living people are born from the dead no less than dead people from the living…'* Surely, he asks, that is sufficient evidence that the souls of the dead exist somewhere so they can be born again?

But are living people born from the dead, and dead people from the living? Are words playing games with me, turning somersaults and cartwheels? Or standing on sentry duty and not allowing me to pass into Socrates' world of philosophy whose logic here I cannot understand?

I have read somewhere that philosophy is a process of clarification; that the quest into natural science is discoverable, but to say something meaningful in metaphysics is bound to fail, because all attempts involve the impossible task of talking about the abstract. If I had questioned Socrates, would he have turned his gaze on me and been kindly disposed but continued to leave me bemused? If Socrates says so, are you dim not to accept what he says, like the Resurrection of Christ which should be believed because St. Paul said so once, and the Archbishop of Canterbury says so now?

I once attended a weekend of lectures on Plato. The professor delivering the lectures was excellent. Over the course of the weekend, however, we learned that he was a Roman Catholic. The subject of Socrates' belief in the resurrection of the soul came up, and the lecturer said positively that it was his conviction that it was not only the soul but the whole body that was resurrected. The whole body? We were all too polite to question him further on such a statement of belief – the word 'Belief' which is so at variance with 'Knowledge'. This is where 'Faith' comes in, something that I totally lack. The dictionary says that 'Faith' is the strong belief in the doctrines of religion, based on spiritual conviction rather than proof. Define Spiritual Conviction, please!

Socrates next goes on to what I also find impossible to accept, saying that the soul, having recycled itself, returns to a new body together with previous knowledge held by the soul in a former life which will be recycled with it. Learning is a matter of recollection – all knowledge is recollection, he claims. Here, any agreement I might have had with Socrates vanishes altogether.

When Simmias tells Socrates he doesn't go along with all that he's said, Socrates takes stock and cheerfully confesses he, Simmias, could well be right in what he thinks; he asks him to give his opinion on the soul, and Simmias immediately moves on from his puff of air suggestion earlier, to comparing it to the attunement of a lyre. He points out that the attunement is quite unseen and immaterial – very lovely and divine in the tuned lyre, though the lyre and strings themselves are corporeal and touchable. If, though, someone goes and smashes the lyre and snaps the strings, there is no longer a lyre, but the attunement and melody still exist somewhere.

Phaedo (after whom this dialogue is named) and who is recounting Socrates' last hours to a friend of his as he himself was there to the very end, tells his companion how Socrates reacted. '...*often as I've admired Socrates, I never found him more wonderful than when with him then.*' That Socrates had an answer didn't surprise him, but he especially admired the pleasure, kindness and approval with which he had received the argument from the two young men. Also his ability to perceive how their words had affected the others gathered there. And especially he admired Socrates' ability to rally them all as though they'd been fleeing in defeat, and to encourage them to examine the argument with him in more detail.

While the soul is with the body, Socrates says, then the body should serve and allow itself to be ruled by the soul: '...*Don't you think the divine is naturally adapted for ruling and domination, whereas the mortal is adapted for being ruled and for service?*' he asks.

His friends agree, and Socrates sets off in full spate, saying that they can surely conclude from what has been said, that the soul is '...*most similar to what is divine, immortal, intelligible, uniform, indissoluble, unvarying, and constant in relation to itself; whereas the body, in its turn is most similar to what is human, mortal, multiform, non-intelligible, dissoluble, and never constant in relation to itself...*'

In other words, while the dead body disintegrates, he says, the invisible soul departs to some other glorious, pure and invisible place, into the presence of the good and wise God where, if God wills it, his own soul will soon be departing – to the kingdom of the god Hades, no less.

So Socrates, using his imagination, believes he will be going down to Hades, lord of the underworld. Well, why not, if that was what was imagined in those far-off days? He hopes that in Hades he'll meet up with others who've led interesting lives. Yet he has every reason to feel pessimistic – he must have been familiar with the story in Homer's *Odyssey*: Odysseus, by means of a magic formula, meets with the souls of the dead who rise up from Hades to speak to him. He is confronted by the soul of King Agamemnon and is shocked to learn he has recently been murdered by his wife. The king throws himself ghostlike into Odysseus' arms, lamenting his fate, but there is no strength to him, nothing of his former strong physique.

Odysseus also meets the soul of Achilles who asks Odysseus how he can bear to come down to Hades where the senseless dead are mere …*imitations of perished mortals*. And the hapless Achilles bewails his death: he would rather be alive even if a slave following a plough, than dead and a king of all the souls in the underworld. Such was the memorable and gloomy picture Homer painted of souls in the afterlife.

Socrates, however, remains determinedly cheerful and optimistic at the prospect of seeing what the next world will bring. Humorously, he declares he is singing his swan-song, but it is his belief that swans never sing out of grief as they approach death, but sing joyfully at the prospect. In other words Socrates refuses to be gloomy, preferring optimism to its depressing opposite, pessimism. In this we are of one mind.

Phaedo, we are told in Plato's dialogue, was sitting on a stool beside Socrates' bed, and that Socrates gathers his hair in his hands and says to him that probably the next day he, Phaedo, will be cutting off his locks as he will by then be in mourning. He then adds, he will cut off his own hair if the argument they are having doesn't end satisfactorily.

Socrates doesn't want Simmias and Cebes to agree with him in order to humour him at the conclusion of his life, but he does want to get to the truth. '...*You must not allow me, in my enthusiasm, to deceive both myself and you, and go off like a bee leaving its sting behind...*'

And he goes on to admit that he doesn't agree with Simmias' idea that the soul is attunement, because a soul is always in opposition to the body throughout its life: sometimes scolding, sometimes encouraging, always in conversation with the body's desires and passions and its fears, apparently quite distinct and separate from them.

Time, though, is fast running out for Socrates. As the last hour approaches, he takes an overview of the world and becomes unusually lyrical. He speaks as though airborne and looking down on the mountains and pockets of earth, rocks and stones, and a world that is beautified with gold and silver; he speaks of the rivers and streams, the river Styx and the judgement of the dead. And he emphasizes those who have been purified by philosophy who, he thinks will live bodiless for eternity (the Orphic belief).

He rallies his companions, telling them they can all have confidence if, during their lifetimes they have rejected the pleasures of the body, believing such things do more harm than good and if, instead, they have devoted themselves to the pleasure of learning, and humouring their souls with temperance, justice, courage, truth and liberality.

Speaking purely personally, considering all the temptations that have come my way, I don't think I've done too badly in humouring my soul. Have I achieved temperance? Well, up to a point. Justice? I've always tried to be fair and don't believe in picking fights. Courage?

Would like more. Truth? Decidedly truthful, but I believe discretion to be important, and tend more and more to tell white lies. Learning? Yes, in what I find interesting – is it my 'inner voice' guiding me in what I get enthusiastic about? Liberality? I could be more charitable, and am not extravagant, though Harry might disagree.

For instance, when he was sorting out his bills one wet afternoon, and I'd just mentioned that Socrates for the good of his soul had possessed only one cloak and went about barefoot, Harry had deliberately selected a sheet of printed paper which he'd held up.

"Something you could well remember next time you go shopping," he'd said. "For the good of your soul there was surely no need for your body to have had – umm – one pair of shoes – seventy quid!" He ran his finger down the tell-tale print. "One velvet jacket – phew! And one hellishly expensive hat!"

"On the contrary," I said, rising at my soul's bidding, "for the good of my body, there was every need. Besides, you said I looked good dressed up for once."

"And so you did. But you'd look just as good without such wild extravagance."

I held my ground. "To buy good shoes, a jacket and hat, and to dress up occasionally, is not only good for my body, but very good for my soul, so there! Blame your niece – she was the one wanting that smart wedding!"

And so the subject ended.

Socrates has now said all he can regarding the body and the soul's survival for which, I fear, my soul will be recycling. He now calmly declares he thinks it's time to take a bath before he drinks the hemlock, as it will save a women having to wash his corpse when he's dead.

His great friend Crito – the one who wanted to pay to get him released, and was prepared to support him if he would agree to live in exile – asks him what instructions he has regarding the care of his children.

His children? Socrates' response is, perhaps, not surprising. All that is needed, he says, is for Crito and all those present to set an example of temperance and all the virtues he has already listed. If they themselves all live virtuously, they can do nothing better for his children who will follow their example. But if they fail to live up to his ideal, they will have failed his children.

Crito reassures Socrates that he will try to do as he says. He then asks about how he wants to be buried. To this Socrates laughs quietly and says to the others that Crito's already seeing his dead body. Well, he can bury him however he thinks most proper because he himself will have gone off.

With that Socrates goes to take his bath, and Crito follows him. After his bath, his three sons, which includes the elder Lamprocles (the one who'd been told to be grateful to his mother), accompanied by the women of the household, are brought to him and, after informing them of his final wishes (we're not told what they are), he asks them to be taken away.

The prison official responsible for his execution enters anxiously. He tells Socrates that if he becomes angry and curses him, he won't reproach him like he reproaches other victims who struggle against death, because he knows it is against those who prosecuted him, and those members of the jury who found him guilty that Socrates feels anger, not him. Well, he says, Socrates knows why he has come:

'*...try to bear the inevitable as easily as you can...*', are his final words, and he turns away to conceal his tears.

But Socrates has seen his emotion, and tells his friends what a civil fellow the man has always been. To shed tears on his behalf? How strange! But now it's time for the hemlock to be brought to him.

There must have been windows to his cell because Crito remarks that there is still time as the sun is on the mountains and hasn't yet gone down. But Socrates can see no point in delaying any longer. He will only be earning ridicule if he clings any longer to life. And he tells Crito to get on with it and do as he asks.

Someone once said to me: "Make the most of your life because you're a long time dead." Harry and I are already much older than Socrates when he died, and the woman's words are very real to me. 'Use the moment' has become my watchword.

How often, when at our weekly market, have I heard snatches of gossip as I've moved between the stalls – unfinished sentences, such as:

'Three days 'e lay there, and nobody...'

'...Died in her sleep, she did, poor soul.'

'...He'd been feeling poorly, but you'd never have thought...'

I can imagine the market gossip when Harry or I join Socrates in death. Of Harry they'd say: 'How the poor man worked! But he made a proper job of that farm, dear man.'

And of me, they'd say: 'She were found slumped over 'er computer, they tell me!'

The man who is to administer the poison to Socrates is called in, and Socrates asks him amiably how he should take it. The man says that after drinking it all, he should then walk about till his legs begin to feel heavy.

Phaedo, who is recounting these events to his friend, tells him how Socrates calmly takes the cup without a tremor and, looking the man in the eye, asks if he should first pour a libation to some god. He is told that the cup only holds just enough to do the job intended, and anything less will leave him still alive, so more will have to be prepared for him. Best to drink all of it in one go, he is told.

He will pray to the gods instead then, Socrates says; he will ask that the removal from this world to the next will be happy. So be it.

With these words he drinks the poison. Everyone present is in tears. Only Socrates remains serene. He reproves them gently, saying the reason he sent his family away was to avoid such distress, and implores them to remain calm and be strong.

Having walked about a little, Socrates declares that his legs are beginning to feel heavy, so he lies down on the bed. The man who gave him the hemlock to drink, examines his legs and pinches his foot to see if Socrates can feel anything. He is told that he can't. Then moving upwards, he pinches him higher up the leg; it becomes clear that the hemlock is working because Socrates feels nothing. He is told that when it reaches his heart it will be the end.

By the time the numbness and cold is in the region of his abdomen, Socrates speaks for the last time: *'Crito…we owe a cock to Asclepius: please pay the debt, and don't neglect it.'*

Crito agrees to fulfil Socrates' dying wish, and he asks if there is anything else Socrates would like him to do for him? But there is no more life left, and the great philosopher is already dead. With great sadness Crito closes his eyes.

CHAPTER 9

ASCLEPIUS
GOD OF MEDICINE AND HEALING

Before finally finishing Socrates' story, a little should be written about why Socrates' last words were about sacrificing a cock to Asclepius.

Asclepius, son of Apollo, was god of medicine and healing.

Asclepius' most famous sanctuary is on mainland Greece at Epidaurus where legend has it he was born. Greek enthusiasts will know of the great open-air theatre at Epidaurus in the Peloponnese between Mycenae and the seaside town of Nauflio. The amphitheatre is a major tourist attraction, and visitors arrive by the coachload to 'oooh' and 'aaah', while their tour-guides display its astonishing acoustics. There, even the sound of a small coin dropped, or the tearing of a piece of paper, can be heard from the highest tiered stone seat (thirty tiers in all, seating forty thousand people). Today dramas are still performed there in the summer months.

Asclepius' sanctuary was designed as a therapeutic centre. It aimed to heal, not just the afflicted part of the body, but the mind and spirit too, hence the amphitheatre, stadium, gymnasium and spiritual buildings.

The sick who came for healing would, after ritual purification, spend the night within the *abaton* close to the temple of Asclepius. There it was expected that during the night each patient would be visited by the god himself, or would receive a curative remedy in a dream. Sometimes the cures were brought about by yellow serpents sacred to Aslepius, and found only within his sanctuary. Rather strangely, they were nocturnal and were said to slither up to the patient in the night and lick the wound which would by morning be miraculously healed.

Various inscriptions have been found there giving details of some of the miracles which have occurred. There was, for instance, a young man who'd come with a spear-head embedded in his jaw; after a night in the *abaton* he'd found by morning that he was holding the spear-head and his jaw was healed. Another inscription recorded an eyeless man who'd found next day that he had eyes.

Asclepius even raised Hippolytus, son of Theseus, from the dead. That Asclepius dared tamper with the laws of nature greatly angered Zeus, and he flung a thunderbolt at Asclepius which reputedly killed this son of Apollo though, being immortal, legend has it he never really died but continued to bring about miraculous cures at his various sanctuaries.

In art Asclepius is depicted carrying a rod with a snake coiled around it. Either the symbol of a snake was used because of the yellow snakes in his sanctuaries, or because snakes slough their skins which represents rebirth and rejuvenation. It is interesting that in the Old Testament Moses had a staff with a bronze serpent wrapped around it, which had only to be looked at to cure venomous snake bites. Curiously, or perhaps it is not really so surprising, a snake coiled around a rod is to this day the symbol of doctors and the medical world, and features on the flag of the World Health Organisation.

★

Another important centre of Asclepius was on the Aegean island of Kos. The Greek physician Hippocrates was born c.460 B.C. on the island, and Socrates would certainly have heard of him. His father was an Asclepiad (a physician/priest) who served at the great Asclepeion sanctuary there.

Hippocrates is mainly remembered for his Hippocratic Oath which in his day went as follows: *I swear by Apollo, the Physician, by Asclepius, by Hygiea and Panacea* (daughters of Asclepius) *and by all the gods and goddesses, making them my witnesses, that I will carry out, according to my ability and judgement, the oath and this covenant...* etc. Today it begins in true Christian style: *With gratitude to God, faith in Christ Jesus, and dependence on the Holy Spirit, I publicly profess my intent to practise medicine for the glory of God...* The Muslims take the oath by praising Allah and swearing to do their best as physicians to serve *...mankind, poor or rich, literate or illiterate, Muslim or non-Muslim, black or white, with patience and tolerance, with virtue and reverence, with knowledge and vigilance, with Thy love in our hearts and compassion for Thy servants, Thy most precious creation.*

Even as a young man Hippocrates' fame must have spread rapidly, because Pericles sought his help in 430 B.C. when Athens was suffering from the plague – Hippocrates was about thirty and Socrates would have been roughly six years older. When the plague subsided several years later, Pericles honoured Hippocrates at the Great Panathenaea festival by crowning him with a golden wreath; he also awarded him free meals for life in the Prytaneum, which was what Socrates said at his trial he thought he deserved rather than execution.

Hippocrates was the first to focus on medicine as a science, and to brush aside ill-health as being a divine punishment. He believed there was a natural cause for disease, and he opposed the Asclepiad priest/physicians who held on to the traditional idea that ill-health was chastisement from on high.

Hippocrates wrote an essay entitled *On Airs, Waters, Places* which was full of fatherly advice and concern, describing how climate and the changing seasons, environment and diet all played a part in the good or bad health and well-being of an individual. 'Excess of any kind is an enemy of nature' was one of his maxims, echoing that of Apollo at Delphi: 'Nothing in excess'.

Hippocrates was a great believer in nature, claiming that nature was untaught and unfailing in itself. *Nothing arises without its natural cause*, he wrote. He recognized that in every human being there were vital forces and energies that functioned naturally to keep a person healthy: digestive organs, heart and blood circulation, lungs for inhaling and exhaling, reproductive organs, brain and nervous system and so on. An imbalance in any one of these causes ill-health and loss of energy. When one thinks about it, it is a miracle that anyone remains healthy and fit, or alive even.

"Don't you think it odd," I once said to Harry, "that when the human body was evolving it didn't just die out?"

"Nothing odd about it," Harry said.

"But not to have a proper functioning liver? Not to have a perfect digestive system? Were these evolving humans in severe discomfort? Were these primordial beings in a lot of pain?"

"It took millions of years to evolve," said Harry, the God-believer who was also a Darwin-fan. At the time he was working on his VAT returns, using a ruler and pen to draw lines of columns on a new page in his hard-back VAT book.

Curiously, I (the God-doubter) found myself saying: "Surely, there just has to have been some sort of divine intervention to get perfection? After millions of years the body wouldn't suddenly say to itself 'Hold it right there, that's exactly IT! Surely, there has to have been a God involved?"

But the God-believer, who was drawing his last column with extreme care, merely said: "It took millions and millions of years," as though doubling up on it made it more acceptable.

"All right, then," I, the God-doubter, said, "explain human consciousness to me."

"Consciousness? Ummmm."

"Consciousness must surely mean some sort of divine magic wand?"

But the God-believer and Darwin-fan was intent on his VAT entries and merely muttered, "Haven't a clue."

"Consciousness, may I say, is something that not even Richard Dawkins can explain," I added. And I picked up Richard Dawkins' book *Science in the Soul* and read out a passage I'd marked: '*...I am less confident about what is for me, as for most biologists, the outstanding scientific problem that remains: the question of how the human brain works, especially the nature of subjective consciousness...*'

There was no answer, and I was left mulling over the annoying unanswered question of the day.

★

Miraculous healings happen today also – not by sleeping in the ancient sanctuaries, but in certain Greek Orthodox churches. Certainly people flock to the island of Tinos to the Church of Panagia Evangelistria, the reason being that the church has a miracle-working icon of the Virgin Mary. The icon is believed to have been painted by St. Luke himself – St. Luke, the physician. Coincidence?

Visitors to the island will see pilgrims on their hands and knees crawling up from the port to the church, several hundred metres on its hill above. They perform this act of humility, either in gratitude for a cure, or to supplicate the Virgin Mary. On reaching the heavily bejewelled icon displayed under glass at the entrance, these stalwarts rise stiffly to their feet, make the sign of the cross, and reverently kiss the icon, mission accomplished.

On the eve of the 15th of August, the feast-day of the Assumption of the Virgin Mary, invalids come from all parts of the Orthodox world, to spend the night in the church gallery. I once spoke to a woman whose daughter, after a night in the gallery and the passing over her head of the sacred icon, had been cured of severe eczema, and a man whose stone-deaf relative had regained his hearing.

Oddly enough I, the God-doubter, am a great believer in the power of the mind. When a close relative, a young mother with small children, had a brain tumour and suffered from partial paralysis, I felt I must do whatever I could. I had a valuable sapphire ring I'd inherited from my mother, and I made a silent vow to the Virgin Mary (in whom I didn't really believe), that if the relative died, then I would sell the ring and give the money to the family, but if she survived, I would send the ring to the Church of

Panagia Evangelistria as a gift.

The young mother did survive and, with the crisis over, I argued with myself that I didn't really have to part with the ring. I hadn't told Harry because I knew he (the great believer) would think I was out of my mind. Yet I knew also I had made that silent vow, and the Virgin Mary knew I had made it. I was, therefore, duty-bound to fulfil my promise. So I wrote a letter to the Church asking them to pray for the relative, and enclosed the ring. Several weeks later, I received a letter of thanks, and the assurance that prayers were being said for the continual recovery of the mother.

Yes, it was a miracle that she survived and was able to continue caring for her family. And, perhaps, even more of a miracle that Harry never once enquired what had happened to that ring!

But enough of that!

So did Socrates' friend Crito sacrifice a cock to Asclepius as Socrates had asked him to? Almost certainly he did. It was customary to sacrifice a cock to this god of healing on recovering from some illness or disability. Cocks herald a new dawn, and it is thought that Socrates saw death as a release from the pain and stresses of this world. With death a new dawn was breaking for him.

EPILOGUE

And so to the airport for our final flight home from Athens. In the departure lounge I find myself seated by a 'poor thing' with a crutch. She is very confiding. Has she had a good holiday, I ask? Yes, they holiday twice a year on the island of Aegina, she replies. But she suffers, she says. It's the arthritis in her hips and her knees. She's had all the replacements, she says, but she now suffers from 'crowns'. She has trouble with her teeth, I ask politely? No, 'crowns', dear. 'Crowns' – trouble down below, you know. It means I'm taken short, so have always to be near a toilet. Oh, yes? I voice my commiseration, and ask her if she enjoys lying on the beach. Oh, she never goes to the beach, she says, she sits on her balcony.

I admire her courage in flying anywhere, and I nod at her husband who also has the courage to come away with her.

I am also aware of how fortunate Harry and I are in being in good health. How, despite my expectations of total failure, of some terrible calamity befalling us while on our travels, we've remained fit and full of energy.

How close we've been to near-disasters, though! The occasion, for instance, when travelling by bus to Epidaurus from Athens and catching sight of the driver's head falling forward, jerking up and falling forward again as sleep overcame him. In his rear-view mirror I could see his eyes drooping and, for a brief while, close. From my seat immediately behind I didn't like to step forward and whisper in his ear, or shout 'Oy!' Was it divine intervention that kept the bus from veering off down a precipice – a divine hand on the steering wheel keeping the bus on course? Perhaps the icon of a saint and a medallion of the Virgin Mary dangling on the dashboard helped?

I'd nudged Harry seated beside me and pointed to the sleeping driver. For some obscure reason, Harry didn't seem too bothered – when abroad he never likes to cause a fuss. Fortunately, the driver's head had jolted up again – it had only been a short nap.

Or on another occasion, was it my guardian angel that had saved me from cracking my skull in a fall? I'd been coming down a sloping concrete path and had missed a shallow step. Seeing me pitch forward, Harry had put out an arm and, instead of catching me, had hurled me over, so I'd crashed down on my back. 'The end! Finality! Death!' my subconscious had screamed at me, as I felt my skull crack. But I'd picked myself up and, apart from a swelling on the back of my head and some niggling pains at the base of my spine, I seemed to be all right.

Afterwards, I was almost grovelling in gratitude to whatever it was that had prevented me from ending up in hospital. Hands together, repeating endlessly: 'Thank you God! Oh, thank you!' There was I, the God-doubter, yet again giving thanks!

Yes, I have a major problem with belief, and I remain a hopeless waverer. As Harry likes to say, I am 'contrary'. When faced with a true believer, I become mulishly atheistic; equally, when someone enforces his atheism on me, I totally reject his no-God arguments.

Our flight is called, and the 'poor thing' with her crutch gets herself slowly to her feet. Yet again I'm reminded of my good fortune, and the words 'There but for the grace of God go I' come into my mind.

God again! Whatever my beliefs are (and Belief is not the same as Knowledge), or whatever the Beliefs of Socrates were, or anybody else's are or were, the word 'God' rises to the surface repeatedly like bubbles of air through mud and water – the breath of life.

APPENDIX

BATTLE OF THE COWSHED

Words! Men are the victims of them! Men are the dupes, the pawns, the puppets of these small, ethereal creatures. It isn't men who make themselves dictators, words do; nor men who make themselves out stupid, only words. Look at politicians! Look at reporters, at writers, academics, lawyers! What are they all? The prisoners of words! They are what words have made them; they are their slaves!

What is history? Nothing but words. What is philosophy? Words. Theology? Words. What is an 'enemy'? What are 'commands'? All words! It is because of words men kill each other. No man would risk his life if words did not force him to it; if words did not stir him into action, did not seize him by the scruff and launch him into battle.

This is a tale of how words used the farmer and his wife. How Gossip came into the neighbourhood and pumped the local jaws so that words flowed; how Gossip turned the people this way and then that to spot the farmer and his wife, and then the farmer's wife with someone else, and then the farmer too and – but that is the story of the

Battle of the Cowshed...

So to begin –

When they were married the word Beef occupied the farmer's mind like a great conqueror and into the fields came bullocks, steers and heifers. For months the farmer's wife, booted and anoraked, aproned and scarfed, stood by her husband, cold but loyal in the autumn mists, the wind and rain. She fed small calves, mixed milk, scattered straw, distributed hay. Loyalty and Devotion wrapped themselves about her and made her out a willing slave – for the time being anyway.

One day the farmer's wife was disturbed by a number of small Question Marks. These Question Marks came dancing by, gyrating gracefully and pirouetting elegantly on their toes before her. Each one begged an answer: would the cattle cease to graze if she pursued some other occupation? Could the farmer not take nails and staples from a paper-bag instead of from her hand? Could her place in lanes and open gateways not be taken by a gate or hurdle? If the farmer wanted something living and companionable why not the cattle-dog instead of her?

The Question Marks danced and pirouetted before her until, quite suddenly, Scholarship arrived and laid a grave hand on her brow, and took her off indoors to study Greek. Words harried her, all shapes and sizes of them: long ones, short ones, modern ones and ancient ones, all demanded her attention. And when they tired of being read in print like soldiers on parade, or of propagating themselves magically from the tip of her pen, then they slid into her mind and amused themselves like children racing round a playground.

And while she grappled with these words indoors, the farmer went about his business outside. Determination clung to his head like a large sombrero hat. Thanks to Determination, the farmer could easily unload ten tons of fertilizer bags, followed by two tons of cattle-cake, followed by a thousand land-drains – all this without the least fatigue. As easily, with Scholarship's assistance, the farmer's wife could write ten thousand words, read the titles of two tons of books, learn fifty words in Greek, cover several miles of print, and show no sign of strain at all. And so time passed.

But, while they were thus occupied, there came into the neighbourhood a diplomat, an old and trusted friend of Passion, who was at this time on a long vacation having been shot in the leg by a Middle Eastern terrorist.

The wife of the diplomat hated Passion; Prude was her constant companion; and Prude often drew her compressed lips and gaunt figure in the image of her own likeness.

Because of his wife's aversion and the diplomat's enjoyment of him, Passion sometimes took his friend beyond the reaches of his home – which was understandable enough.

One day the diplomat felt Passion urging him to fresh adventures and so, without delay, he went limping to the library to exchange his books for others more appropriate to his present mood. Expectation and Ecstasy flew before him like two outriders drawing him along. He limped after them elegantly with the aid of a stout walking-stick; and everywhere he went eyes followed him: he always looked a diplomat amongst the rabble mob.

At the library, at the sound of a stout stick striking the floor boards, the farmer's wife looked up from her Greek lexicon and saw the diplomat. At the sight of the Greek lexicon open on the library table, the diplomat looked down and saw the farmer's wife. He found a seat nearby, opened his book and fixed his eyes to the text. Expectation and Ecstasy flew back and forth between them, creating a strong magnetic pull. But the diplomat was not a diplomat for nothing; although he knew at once that he was destined, he appeared only to be studying his book. Similarly, the farmer's wife, aware of the elegant addition to the readers in the room, continued to copy out her alpha, beta, gamma, delta as though nothing else interested her.

In time they met – not in the library as might have been supposed but, as it seemed by chance out hunting. Scholarship, growing weary one day, allowed Diversion to take the farmer's wife out following the hounds on foot. And there she saw the sporting diplomat leaning on his stick with his binoculars lifted to his eyes. A mutual friend, seeing each glancing at the other, soon introduced them both.

And Gossip was out hunting too. Yes, Gossip glanced at Passion toying with the diplomat; and Gossip saw how Pleasure lit the object of his eye and made her glow. And Gossip turned the locals all about, and made them play the game of 'Spot the Diplomat and farmer's wife'.

And all the while the farmer was at work. Beneath the large sombrero of Determination, the farmer drove his pick into the ground to find blocked drains; and drove it in again to search for leaking water-pipes in fields. He drove his spade into the earth to dig out ditches, and drove in fencing stakes and gate posts. And when he wasn't driving things like that he drove in nails or drove the tractor or drove cattle from one pasture to another helped by his faithful cattle-dog. And every evening Determination sat him down and kept him busy with his bills, although he seldom paid them: he merely shuffled them and looked at them. Sometimes he added them all up and gulped, before he shuffled them some more.

And every evening now the farmer's wife spoke Greek to him, and he talked Beef back at her. To be blunt neither listened to the other. And so the farmer never heard her say she'd met a diplomat, nor she that he had dug two holes to find a leaking water-pipe. He never heard her tell him she'd seen him in the library first, and met him later at the local meet; nor did she hear the farmer say he'd found the pipe at last and cut and fitted a new joint. Nor did the farmer hear her tell him that a mutual friend had introduced them both, and now had asked them out to dine; nor did she hear the farmer say that he had found another swamp and this must mean another leak, and it must be a rotten pipe.

And so it came about that not long afterwards the farmer and his wife, the diplomat and his wife too, and several other agricultural people, found themselves by candle-light around the dinner-table.

And while the others spoke of rats and mice and moles and blight; of foxes, fences, riding, falling, good and bad weather, the diplomat (seated to the right of the farmer's wife) sat sleek and suave, and spoke of elegance and anarchy, of columns, domes and temples; of the Aegean sea and highjackers and terrorists. Passion played about the features of this sporting diplomat, and drew the face of the farmer's wife towards him. And, as the meal progressed, and the wine warmed and animated them, they never heard the others speak of cows and sheep and digging holes and mending leaks in water-pipes; of high market prices and low ones; of dead animals and live ones and vet bills; but only what they themselves discussed such as the merits of a bygone age; of modern times and drama; of art and exhibitions; of opera and books. And Passion drew the head of the farmer's wife a shade nearer still.

But then something happened to cast a shadow over the party. The diplomat's wife, whose thin lips were being held compressed by Prude, was visited by Jealousy. Yes, there was Jealousy whose horrid light cast a green glow into the woman's eyes. And Jealousy made her two green eyes, like two round saucers, stare at the diplomat and farmer's wife until Etiquette intervened and made the farmer's wife turn to her companion on her left. Soon she too was chatting about autumn leaves and summer flowers; of cattle dogs, terriers, fleas and worming powders; of warble fly and drenches; of barley beef and mangel-wurzels. And the diplomat turned to his companion on his right and spoke of acreage and arable; of hounds and hunting, foxes and pheasants; of rat poison and seed potatoes. And so long as they both talked to their neighbours on the other side, Jealousy receded, only to be seen when they turned towards each other once again.

And so the evening passed. The wife of the diplomat was first to leave, pleading her husband's bullet-ridden leg as the excuse to go home early (doctor's orders she explained). Always the diplomat, her husband did not demur but limped off after her, gracefully leaning on his stick. But then, you see, he'd gleaned some information: every Tuesday, he now knew, the farmer went to market leaving his wife at home. And he nestled this small piece of information secretly against his heart. Yes, he nestled it comfortably in his breast.

Next day the farmer's bank statement came through the post (he and his wife had a joint account). At once Anxiety seized him and he accused his wife of profligacy which made her break two plates while washing up. Words such as Irresponsible and Extravagance flew from his mouth and struck her hard like rubber bullets. She stuttered like a stengun in response, and pointed out he got the bills, not her. When did she ever buy calf-nuts or cattle-cake, gadgets or machinery, she demanded? Wasn't he the one who bought in calves and bought dried milk, fertilizer bags and hurdles, buckets, drain-pipes, nails and tractor tyres and pitchforks, spades and shovels? Why blame her, when all she did was read or write or study Greek? She never spent a thing, she said.

Determination sat round and unflappable on the farmer's head while his wife voiced this opinion. But Anxiety made him speak again. He pointed out that what he did was for the good of both of them and what she did was not; to which she at once retorted that she did the housework and carried out many small requests at inconvenient moments like any servile half-besotted slave; and she only studied Greek when all this work was done. Yes, she would like to go to Greece, she said, to visit Delphi, Corinth and, of course, to see the Parthenon; but had she bought a ticket yet? No, she had not.

But Anxiety made the farmer now produce a carrier-bag from which he drew an invoice, and he asked her for an explanation. She nearly broke another plate. That, she told him, was for the dress she'd bought to wear the night before. She had, she said, told him about it; she had, she said, even worn it; she'd even asked him if he'd liked it; but he had been so taken up with water-pipes and leaks and drinking-troughs, punctures, diesel oil and anti-freeze, that he hadn't heard a word she'd said, or seen what she'd been wearing. The farmer thumbed the cheque-book stubs, and turned up several further purchases which made him choke as though he'd swallowed several fish-bones. All his wife said then was that she'd thoroughly enjoyed the dinner and feeling elegant for once, and hang the expense!

Now there was in the neighbourhood a blonde of great allure, a friend of the farmer's wife. This blonde would sometimes come up to the farm to see her friend but, finding her not there, she'd help the farmer with his work instead. She was a girl just bursting with Enthusiasm. She loved farms, loved animals, loved tractors and mechanical diggers, and anything that needed to be fed or oiled. It was Enthusiasm brought her up and the farmer liked Enthusiasm.

The following Tuesday (market day) the blonde of great allure (Enthusiasm being what it was) asked if she could hitch a lift to town riding in the cattle-lorry. The farmer readily agreed, believing she could help him load and unload two fat bullocks which he hoped to sell. But as they set off on the road together, who should occupy their persons in the cab but three bad words. These words at first pretended to be Friendship, Trust and good Sense; but no sooner were they on their way they threw off their disguise and showed themselves for what they really were: Thrill, Ogle and Seduction. And all the way to market the three bad words teased and played about the farmer and the blonde, making them experience very pleasurable sensations.

Meanwhile the diplomat was coming to the farm; he did not feel his bullet-wound at all, so much was Passion playing with his thoughts. And flying along with him came Sin who, being only three letters, could easily slip into the minds of mortals.

The farmer's wife was in the yard when the diplomat arrived. She had been feeding calves, and he relieved her of a bucket and pressed a book into her hands – a book on ancient Greece, a book he thought she'd like. And so she took him in and sat him down, and stuck her nose into the book then asked all sorts of boring things about the marvels of that distant age, things far removed from the more pressing problems of the moment.

The diplomat sat gallantly nearby while Passion sent sparks flying from his eyes. But Sin, having no patience with such scholarly pursuits, soon dived from the head of the diplomat into the deep waters of the female mind, sending ever widening circles of meaning into her expression, until the poor woman quite forgot what she was saying.

The diplomat was expert at such times. He recognized the signs at once and gave himself up to the occasion. With a knowing smile he left his seat, dropped his stick and advanced like Zeus in a shower of gold to capture Danae.

And now Time flew – sometimes that happens: Time, contrary to human wishes, flies, while on occasions when Time would only fly, then Time stands still. But now Time flew and the farmer and the blonde were already driving back from market. Enthusiasm had caught them both and Determination was nowhere to be seen. And all the while the three bad words were playing wickedly about them.

As the farmer turned into the driveway he saw an unfamiliar car, muttered "damned visitor!" and drove on up to the top yard to keep out of the way. There he embraced the blonde and, urged on by the three bad words, he embraced her once again and led her to the cowshed.

Now Trouble came. He always lurked about where management was slacking off and, it has to be admitted that the farmer and his wife were both preoccupied with matters far from agricultural at that time. So Trouble came and, seeing two untied hurdles in the yard, he urged some bullocks past them into the big-bagged silage. Once there they tore the heavy-duty plastic with their teeth, climbed the bags and ravaged every one of them. Up came the cattle-dog snapping at their tails and Trouble, like a great egg-whisk, whipped them all up until they were a frenzied whirl of hooves, split bags, mud, slurry, flying fur and teeth. Over went the hurdles, and the bullocks, with their tails aloft, broke from the yard and away, away, away –

And now the farmer heard the bellowing bullocks. "God! you blind fool!" he yelled (the farmer meant himself but the girl did not know this), and he left the cowshed in one bound. Emotion, who'd been hovering above the blonde fell like a stone into her open mouth and lodged like a gob in her throat, threatening to choke her. Immediately she gave a strangled cry, but the farmer never heard, nor did he once look back. No, with Trouble there he was already running to the house with one thought in his mind: he must fetch his dear wife to help.

Indoors the diplomat was whispering sleekily into the ear of the farmer's wife: soft words conveying to her many things. The farmer's wife grew beautiful as though she were a work of art rather than a farmer's mate. His lips engaged her ear, and now he whispered that his bullet-wound necessitated that he rest his leg and when did she expect the farmer back from market?

But as he spoke the words, quite suddenly they all blew back into his face and scattered in the air like specks of dust dancing on a sunbeam. Looking at the farmer's wife, he saw Distraction scattering her wits and Shock pull up her brows like catapults. Turning towards the object of her gaze, he saw the farmer at the window peering in. How much could the farmer see? He did not wait in order to be told, but tore himself neatly from the farmer's wife, much as a shredder tears secret information when an embassy's in flight. As he did so, four words flew from the farmer's mouth: "Bullocks in the silage!"

Never had the diplomat handled a farmer's wife before. Instead of the soft, rounded female form the four words 'Bullocks in the silage!' produced a tightly sprung coil; instead of the quiet, caressing voice that charmed, came a klaxon pitched two octaves higher. This schizophrenic creature, no longer the princess, spat a great oath from her mouth like a peach-stone, sprang like a frog from his grasp and was gone.

Two seconds later he saw five bullocks in the yard. He saw the farmer's wife dash past the window half in and half out of her gum-boots but pulling at them as she ran; and then he saw her stop. Why? Why did she stop dead and stare at something up the yard? Disbelief pulled down her jaw and made her gape. But soon the bullocks in a bunch moved off and she gave chase again. He saw the farmer leaping forward with a stick to block one exit, then springing to another to block that, before hurling the stick towards his wife who caught it on the run as together they vanished after their livelihood.

A moment passed and then the blonde of great allure came into view. She stumbled down the yard buttoning her clothes, and fled past the farmhouse choking from Emotion, her face averted. She was hoping to go unobserved, but was clearly seen. Soon she was gone as well.

Disappointment, like a wet flannel, covered the face of the despairing diplomat. He sat, or rather slumped, down on a chair. At times he held his head in his hands, at times he ran his fingers through his hair, and at other times he moved a hand over his noble features. Sin and Passion now were far away. Had he only been a pawn, used by Passion in some game, he wondered? Could Sin so quickly occupy his mind, only to depart as swiftly when a bunch of bullocks got into the silage? A diplomat and farmer's wife, was it so foolish? At last he heaved a heavy sigh and rose and found his stick and left.

Later that evening, in the warm comfort of his home, Prude offered him his wife's thin cheek to kiss; its meagre familiarity comforted him a little. But a slight whiff of dung made the woman's nostrils flare. At once Prude sat his wife down and proceeded to open and shut her mouth as if it were a cat-flap through which questions leapt. Taking courage from a glass of Scotch, the diplomat replied with suitably slick sentences designed to satisfy her curiosity. Prude, of course, did not believe a word of it and, taking his wife to bed early, soon had her fast asleep and snoring her contempt.

Back on the farm the *Battle of the Cowshed* was imminent. The bullocks had been rounded up, the big-bagged silage all re-bagged. The time was after ten o'clock at night. And, as the farmer fed hay to the small calves and his wife shovelled nuts to them, armies of words: verbs, nouns adjectives and adverbs, were circling round and round the confined space of their two heads. Suspicion had the farmer's troops under his command, whilst Indignation led the wilder bunch of accusations fighting for the farmer's wife.

The first salvo came from the angry woman – straight off the top of her head in a most undisciplined manner. Indignation tried to hold her tongue but without success. "Not to tie the hurdles! what were you thinking of?" A great flash came from the farmer's wife. Metal upon metal rang out as shovel and bucket struck the calf partitions and cattle-rearing nuts went flying through the air. A loose, erratic bunch of words shot from her tongue: "You think I don't know why those bullocks all got out? You think I'm dumb like that blonde bitch?"

Immediately the two armies locked themselves in bitter conflict. The farmer's wife opened up her mouth and a fusillage of words, horrible adjectives, lethal nouns, poured from her: an undisciplined mob of military verbiage. General Suspicion responded on the farmer's side with a thousand gibes and lambasted the woman with small, explosive charges of being unfaithful – disloyal – shameless – untrustworthy – frivolous – foolhardy and useless –

The battle now was at its height; the noise was audible across the valley. Both sides were firing simultaneously; each had the other in his sights and triggered fearful poisoned darts and wounding words: "He made me feel quite feminine again. I liked it!"

"Of course he did. He'd nothing else to do but flirt with you."

"You beast! Don't talk to me of flirting!"

Suddenly from the barrel of the farmer's mouth came a Guffaw. The Guffaw spun through the air and swirled and coiled around the woman opposite like a lassoo: "Ha! You're your mother's daughter all right – always the last word! God! You're funny!"

Now Silence descended, falling quite suddenly between them like a dead bird between two dogs. And Indignation tied the woman's tongue and sealed her lips trying to keep Silence and on the other side Suspicion observed Silence for a while and then seized his opportunity to call a truce. He sent a line of reasonable vocabulary marching out under Major Condescension: "You have to work at marriage if you want it to succeed."

Indignation pulled the woman's face into a fearful scowl: "Work? My God! Haven't I been working?" A second remark aimed at her heart flew from Suspicion's lines: "Believe it or not I love you!" Indignation fired a wild retort: "Love me? Then you've a bloody awful way of showing it!" Two finely pointed sentences flew through the air and now sank home: "If working hard on your behalf is a bloody awful way of showing it, then bloody awful it will have to be. I still LOVE YOU!"

General Indignation felt the puff go out of him and his letters visibly shrank. Blame and Reproach tried to rally some support, but their best nouns and verbs were already in full flight. A stream of words charged straight into their broken lines striking at what followers remained. First Beast and Rotter fell to Tenderness; then Brute and Cad collapsed as Kindness mowed them down; and Fib was chased and killed by Truth, while Extravagance who saw Prudence coming for him, turned and ran back into the head of the farmer's wife.

General Indignation, deflated beyond all recognition, prayed that his reserves would arrive in time; but his array of nouns and verbs and all his best fighters were utterly disseminated. Blame and Reproach tried to work the woman's tongue around two words 'damn you!' but she was altogether inarticulate, and they died together on her lips. Only a few useless stragglers remained such as 'and', 'but', 'so', 'if'. These staggered bravely amongst floundering letters and scattered punctuation marks, before falling in their tracks.

General Suspicion was triumphant. His front line had held and he went forward to victory, the well-trained nouns and verbs marching neatly out in a long, unbeatable sentence: "I love you! Like it or not you are my wife. And as a farmer's wife you ought to know by now the cows come first!"

There was no answering volley, no sharp retort as words

failed the farmer's wife. Instead a white handkerchief was taken out, and she covered her face with it as a symbol of complete surrender.

And so the *Battle of the Cowshed* was written – words saw to it. Such words! Such valiant words! They laid themselves on paper, competing with each other for the honour of a place; each one wanting to contribute to the memory of the one and only battle of its kind: the famous *Battle of the Cowshed*.

GOD AND THE BRAIN

It never occurred to God, no, not once, that he might become mystified, absolutely bamboozled by Man. Man was his creation – a complicated creature of heart and guts and skin and bone and into his head he had stuffed a brain. He hadn't the least idea what that brain was going to conceive – he supposed that, perhaps, it might evolve a sort of language and some poetry, or produce a bit of music and a song or two. He certainly didn't foresee that it would have that voracious appetite for knowledge! exploration! diagnosis! argument! invention! It seemed as if from the very beginning of its creation the brain had set purposefully out to gain dominion over Man and Man had become its proud servant. No one was more astonished than God who, by the twenty-first century was absolutely perplexed by what was going on on earth. God began to hold himself well back out of sight for fear of being thought a bit, well, a bit uneducated.

For a start God was astounded that the brain had discovered that putting two and two together made four; that by playing with numbers it could do all manner of tricks with them; that it could divide them and multiply them and solve equations and – and – and evolve algebra, geometry, trigonometry, and work out fractions and percentages and God knew not what. The whole business of mathematics was a profound mystery to God as he himself had no brain. To create mathematics out of thin air, as it were, was a perpetual wonderment to God – a profound mystery in which he personally had no faith. God wasn't sure that numbers – mathematics – had improved the world. In fact, he rather thought it hadn't because so many of those poor devils (he called men his poor devils, because that was how he saw them), so many of those poor devils tore at their hair and frowned and shook their heads, saying: "God! what a problem! Oh, God! I can't solve this one!" and so on.

Looking down on London God wondered and wondered at all the transport which Man had created for himself thanks to his brain. What had been wrong with the camel, God asked himself? A camel drank water and would kneel down to be mounted, whereas cars wouldn't budge an inch unless men drilled for oil and went to endless trouble to get petrol for them. Cars often crashed, camels never did. Cars had to be manufactured, camels reproduced themselves. And the noise! Poor Man, God thought, had got himself into a terrible muddle with all those cars and double-decker buses and motor-bikes and taxis moving endlessly along the streets of London. And how often did they ask God for his help! "Please, God, help me with this engine!" was their constant prayer. Or, "Please, please God, help me change this wheel so that I can get to the station in time to catch the train which will get me to the airport to catch my plane." Well, what could God do? He hadn't the foggiest about engines. Did the poor devils suppose he had eyes, and fingers and engineering expertise? Did they suppose he had had a training in mechanics? God felt a strong inclination to shift himself back to his desert. He found the wide, undulating sweep of the Sahara more relaxing; there he found pleasure in seeing the occasional oasis glinting like a jewel, and a few bedouin travelling slowly – yes, on camels.

God murmured a prayer to himself and drew back behind a cumulus cloud, totally and completely nonplussed. But soon he was taking another look at this great city – at the rows and rows of houses. God cast his eye over the buildings of London, over all those thousands of terraced houses, and all those blocks of flats and the hundreds of other huge edifices. How, God wondered, had men ever managed to build them? Some of them were hundreds of feet in the air, way above the heads of the poor devils, way out of reach of their hands. Why? How had they done it? God, of course, knew perfectly well what was behind this clobber of concrete and bricks and tarmac and cement-rendering – it was the brain!

When God had made Adam and put him in Paradise there had been no need of houses at all, but then the weather had been balmy and Adam had been able to sleep wherever he had happened to lie down – Eve too, of course. But once they had eaten the fruit of the tree of knowledge, all hell had been let loose and God had had a fearful struggle with the winds and the clouds and everything which had reacted violently as a result of Eve eating the forbidden fruit. From then on the poor devils had had to find shelter for themselves. They had made tents – that's what their brains had first suggested to them, and God had been pleased with the brain then. A tent was something God thought quite a bright idea as anyone with a tent could move it to wherever he wanted to be and put it up again. But houses! A man with a house was tied down to that precise spot on earth and, if he went away he was without shelter. God thought it much better when men had tents and wherever they had gone they had taken their tents and their families and their animals with them, and they had ridden on those camels and had a string of other camels to carry their possessions.

God's attention was drawn to a particular clump of buildings close to the river Thames. God had seen these before – they were the Houses of Parliament. And now he saw the poor devils in session in the House of Commons. And as God watched he was astonished! Where was Solomon's wisdom, he wondered? Why were they all shouting and jeering at each other? There was one man trying to speak but nobody was listening, while another sat importantly alone yelling louder than all the others and shouting 'Order, order!' but nobody was paying attention. Meanwhile, all around Parliament the streets were seething with traffic, and men and women stood staring up at the Houses of Parliament taking photographs. God noticed that a number of policemen were standing guard at the entrance, and God thought the people were quite right to be defending themselves against all those poor devils inside with the best brains.

God withdrew behind his clouds again to mull over what he had perceived. But he couldn't resist another peep at the great city of London. This time he saw a gun-battle and people being killed. It didn't surprise him as the poor devils had always killed each other. God had created stones and in the old days brute force and a good large rock on the head had settled matters; but, then, they had dreamed up gunpowder – God wasn't sure how it had come about, but

APPENDIX 153

the poor devils were forever messing about with this and that until something reacted and there! a new discovery! Now men only had to point this small metal object and phhhhht! bang! somebody fell down dead. God had his thunderbolts and lightning, they were his creations and did his bidding, but Man had this small refined thing he could hide away in his pocket; but then Man was a small beast and all was relative, God supposed. Nevertheless, God wasn't sure that he had created men in order that they should kill each other. God began to tremble a little at the thought of this brain which made all things possible it seemed.

He was about to withdraw into the shadow of his clouds again, completely and totally non-plussed, but he shifted his gaze a fraction of a degree and there! yes, there he perceived those weapons he had so frequently heard spoken of lately – weapons that could destroy whole communities at a time! "Oh, God" was the repeated prayer, "take away these deadly weapons! Please, God, rid us of these nuclear bombs!" as if it was all God's fault that they were there! It was clear that they were considered wickedly important because a number of the poor devils armed to the teeth were standing guard beside them like so many ants. Outside the perimeter fence he'd once seen a bunch of women – looking rather like a pack of wolves, and at sight of them God had thought how the poor devils had come a long way from his Garden of Eden – from Paradise.

God took another look at this city and wondered why so many of the poor devils, instead of living actively seemed to sit limply infront of a box watching other people living. God was most surprised that watching others living seemed to these people more exciting than doing anything for themselves. He wondered why it was that people shot each other a great deal on this box, and many of them made love on the box. And, meanwhile, the watchers just sat and did nothing. Then God saw that on the box appeared pictures – scenes of shootings and bombings which he'd lately witnessed amongst his chosen people in the land he had given them. That was really curious! There it all was just as he had seen it – but on the box. What was even odder was that he saw in one home a poor devil spring up in a rage and shout, "those bloody Arabs!" while next door another covered his face in despair and groaned, "God! those Jews!" God knew exactly how they felt, although he was surprised they showed an interest so far away in London.

God understood, of course, that all these scenes of war and strife were what men called the 'news'. In the past 'news' only came when there was any. Now it seemed that the poor devils were determined to have 'news' whether there was any or not, whether it concerned them or didn't. They filled their heads with everything that had nothing to do with them at all. They listened to a voice which came as it seemed from nowhere at regular intervals, and switched on the picture on the screen to watch a face giving them the 'news'. They also read 'news'papers which told them not only what had happened everywhere in the world but also what hadn't happened. Why did they no longer wait for the future, God wondered? Instead, they had experts who predicted results and gave weather forecasts, while others declared secrets to the whole world and imagined they were still secret: "A secret meeting is being held at… between so-and-so and such-and-such"; "I won't tell you the result as that is secret, but so-and-so has won." God suspected that the brain which showed such capacity for producing the past and unravelling the future would soon make the present altogether redundant, so that the poor devils would barely live at all, but exist in limbo so to speak, while all around would be the past and the future.

Then God remembered that he particularly wanted to take a look at those criminal courts in London – at those who had broken his commandments and had been caught in the act, and at all those who had also broken them but sat in judgement. Yes, there was the Old Bailey. God looked on at one of the trials. He watched the defendant swearing on the Bible and found it a bit comical that a man should be supposed to tell the truth when he'd sworn on the Bible. God didn't concern himself with these criminals. They were entirely the problem of the poor devils on earth. He didn't mind them using his name if it helped to keep them all under control. If only those judges realized how those criminals asked him also for his help: "Oh, Gawd!" they'd cry, "I've made a bleedin' cock-up of this! Christ! tell me 'ow to get out of this one!" Well, God had found that the easiest way of all was to let them all get on with it themselves. Once he interfered then they'd all go into raptures about 'the miracle': "It's a miracle!" they'd keep repeating. They didn't realize that what was a miracle one moment was nothing the next in relation to eternity. God worked miracles occasionally only because it was easier to do so than to put up with a voice begging and begging. How would anyone of them like it if he kept nagging and nagging at him? Sometimes God really wished he hadn't made men so aware of him.

God rather regretted that on the seventh day he had rested. He wished profoundly that he hadn't made a thing about the seventh day. On that day – Sunday – he was pestered with requests and petitions and deafened by church bells ringing, not to mention the poor devils singing hymns and psalms. All their problems came surging up to him and God always helped where he could but, frankly, for the most part he hadn't any idea what the poor devils were talking about. He had absolutely no understanding of finance or nuclear waste or acid rain; absolutely no knowledge of office work or industrial unrest, or of banks and suchlike. God was sorry to be so inadequate, so unequal to Man's modern-day requirements, but it was Man's own fault for complicating his life so completely, and getting himself into the muddle he was in. God could only be blamed for setting the ball rolling, so to speak, in the first place. Now he only hoped that the brain could find a way out of the tangle into which it had got itself.

Then God heard the first peel of bells and knew that, yes, it must be Sunday again. The sound of the bells rose up to him from all quarters of London. God took some thick wisps of cloud and stuffed them into his ears to stop himself from being deafened. Then he sank down behind his cumulus cloud and considered the matter of that brain. How would it all end, he wondered? Men thought that he, God, knew everything, which of course was nonsense because he hadn't a brain. What did concern him now, though, was something he had lately discovered: the poor devils had recently invented of all things, yes! a brain of their own making! In the future what they couldn't work out for themselves they would get their computer brain to do for them. God thought the poor devils would live to regret it, just as he himself was regretting their brain.

God relaxed comfortably into the cushion of cloud and tried to think it all out, as well as an eternal mind can think out the mysteries of a brain. Night was falling. God was glad he had created night; it gave him some respite from the poor devils who then all nodded off to sleep. In his view night was one of his better creations. He cast his mind back to the days when he was creating the world. He had thought at the time that it was perfect. Why, he wondered, had Man thought it necessary to change his world so completely? But, then, all creators thought their work perfect until others came along to judge and criticize it. God thought of the labour he had put into the creation of his world. How he had chiselled and chiselled away at his globe to make it perfectly spherical – all right, the poor devils found mountains and chasms and all that, but to God's infinitely greater eye it was a smooth, round world. Had the poor devils seen what God had discarded then they would have had a greater understanding of how much God had done for them. If they had only seen the chippings and the debris in outer space (some of which they called stars) to realize to what lengths God had gone to pare away from the original block in order to expose the pure gem which was their world.

God was feeling the peace of night descending on him again, when all at once – quite suddenly! – he had a very nasty surprise, a really horrible shock! His whole being felt threatened as from nowhere – well, up from earth, in fact – shot a couple of the poor devils heading into the heavens! How dare they! Oh, how could they dare to do that! No, it was too much! To be now invading his air space! He had created birds for fun to show men that it was possible in a limited way to be off the ground and not necessarily always on it, but now the invasion of his heavens!

It was the brain, of course! The brain! the brain! the brain! Oh, how he regretted that brain! God wished and wished he could make a brain for himself. But where would he put it? Where was there a safe and solid corner to lodge a brain when all was eternal and spiritual? Well, of course,

God did have his solution. Yes, there was only one possible way to overcome the problem: he must become Man again. Only by doing that would he ever begin to understand the terrible mess those poor devils were making of his beautiful world he had so carefully created for them.

OLYMPIAN GOD IN MOURNING

For many years Lord Zeus, lord of the ancient world, sat despondent on his throne high up on the peaks of Mt. Olympus. There he pondered his destiny and tugged his beard and knit his brow and drummed his fingers on a nearby rock. His family trod tiptoe around him, much as families do when a member is severely ill and death is a dark shadow ominous and threatening. Some dared to speak – a few words only – so fearful were they that the drumming of the fingers on the rock, which was a warning sign, would stop and repressed anger would suddenly erupt.

At last a day arrived when Lord Zeus with his far seeing eyes raised them to the world about him. He looked first towards the west, towards his ancient sanctuary at Dodona, some miles inland from the sparkling sea thrown like a wrap around the shoulders of the earth. At Dodona the pious had once come seeking his advice, hoping that a spark from his almighty mind would ignite them with new energy to resolve their mortal problems. Lord Zeus remembered how he teased them with his answers, impelling them to interpret as they could the rustling of the leaves in his sacred oak tree. Were not these leaves blown by his holy breath? Did not his oak tree bud and blossom every year through its divine roots spread deeply in the hallowed earth? But now the far- seeing eyes of Zeus gazing on his sacred precincts saw built on it a Christian church. With sorrow he observed how all the votive offerings, given gladly to him by his petitioners in grateful thanks, had been cast pell-mell into an open pit, flung there with triumphant relish and with malice by a Christian priest.

He turned his gaze south-west towards Olympia and saw grimly all the changes there under the Christian emperor. Gone were the Olympic Games which had once been the glorious signal for all warring states to call a truce in order that spectators could in safety flock to see fair combat between athletes. Such things were now forbidden by decree and there too, within the sacred precincts close to his temple was a dedicated basilica to the Christian God.

Turning his far seeing eyes due south a tremor passed through the Olympian frame as Zeus saw the defilement of his daughter's worship by a church built into the Parthenon at Athens. Lord Zeus groaned as his eyes took in the other churches made sacred to Jehovah in other parts of his beloved daughter's city. He groaned and tugged his beard and trembled too as he turned his eyes eastward and saw there at Thessaloniki more Christian basilicas, one dedicated to Agios Demetrius, whose name resembled his own sister's. And, closer still, below him at the holy site of Dion where the great Alexander had once made sacrifice to him, a basilica now stood and worshippers were singing to their God, Jehovah, and praising him for all his works and the creation of the world – as though there was no other God but him.

Lord Zeus, in the deepest gloom, thought over all the past events. How was it men had turned from him? How was it they had turned the focus of their thoughts from life on earth and fretted more about the life to come? Lord Zeus could not comprehend it. For men to welcome death, seeking to be born again to a new life eternal with the Christian God, seemed to Lord Zeus rather odd, to say the least. He had been unable to prevent men hastening to attain salvation when the word spread that the world would soon be at an end and that a Day of Judgement was imminent. All disasters had been 'signs' of Armageddon. And yet the world continued its slow spin. But mankind! these men! these Christians! It was as if their minds were spinning too; as if their heads were in the heavens and their feet had left the earth and had lost contact with reality.

He blamed himself. He should have acted earlier to stop the spread of Christianity. When those men they called Apostles came journeying to Greece speaking 'with tongues' which was a sort of communication, he should have realized that this sort of baying like hounds was not normal. If men were speaking 'with tongues' and others purported to understand the incomprehensible he should have acted then with thunderbolts. Yet at the time he paid no heed to it thinking it a foolish mortal whim which would soon pass. He had not reckoned on the fear men had of everlasting hell with the world's end declared to be so near. He had not reckoned they could understand the incomprehensible or the unbelievable and spread about what they liked to call the 'good news' but which to him, Zeus, was not good news at all but bad news.

Then Zeus smiled. He cast his eye around his family who believed him still to be in mourning, and quickly concealed his smile by lowering his head which gave him an air of ever greater despondency. Yet he smiled grimly, remembering what he had heard about the holy Councils to which the Christian bishops had all gone to argue on the subject of divinity: on the nature of the Son of God and whether the Son was truly God or truly Man or whether his mother Mary had been truly virgin or not quite virgin; whether each was blessed with the Divine Will only or had a Human Will or whether all was ordered by God or by the Holy Ghost or a combination of all or an equation of it, or what? How, Lord Zeus wondered, how was it that those first Christians had spoken 'with tongues' and all had understood without undue explanation, yet the bishops themselves, who could argue with so much vigour and controversy, could understand so little? Why, he wondered, did they try to understand so much at all, when it was not in the human nature to comprehend the divine and the incomprehensible? No priests of his, those laymen who did service at his temples, had wasted time in hot debate about such things as the nature of his sons either born to mortal women, or born from his own head, or about things of which no proof could be unveiled nor ever would be.

That the Roman emperors had deified themselves had been an impudence! He should have flung down thunderbolts and made it known who was god, but for some reason he had not. For some reason he had grown weary with their folly. For some reason he had turned his back on those usurpers of his supremacy and had allowed into the empire those Egyptian gods who had also stolen worship due to him and drawn it instead towards themselves. Yes! he himself had been at fault allowing it! And Lord Zeus gnawed his lip in anger.

He continued smiling grimly as he remembered how he had been glad to see the Christian faith leading men to strange excesses (something frowned on by the Olympian family). Some, for instance, instead of living lives like men and mixing freely with their own kind, had in their Christian zeal separated themselves from their companions. Some sat cross-legged on pillars in a divine state; others lived in caves or perched in trees like birds. And, far from men thinking such things were signs of madness, Lord Zeus had been astonished when he saw the faithful flocking to these solitary ascetics in awe and reverence at their Christian faith. Yes, far from drawing back because they saw such things as lunacy, they instead drew nearer regarding it as the ultimate in human wisdom. Although these holy freaks were dressed in rags and were mere skin and bone, those who came to see them saw beauty; they saw dignity in their indignity and marvelled at the eyes that glowed with fervour or with fever as their bodies were subjected to excesses of endurance in order to be closer to the God they worshipped. It seemed the more they suffered the more all men rejoiced that they could endure it.

But why should they suffer and endure was the question Zeus asked himself? What had got into men that the more they suffered the more did they rejoice in it? How could he, Lord Zeus of Olympus, bring men back to him or return them to their senses when the travails of the abnormal seemed to them more admirable than the normal travails of a daily life? Were they nearer the divine or were they demented beings, Lord Zeus wondered? Had any of his worshippers dared to live aloof in order to draw nearer to him, Zeus, he would have reacted with all power and vigour and found it a good reason to let them know what he thought of them. Under his lordship it had been well known to all mortals that they should live in harmony

– excelling, yes, but not exceeding or striving to be more than men.

And when these holy men had died, as all men must whether holy or unholy, the Christians then had seized their bodies, falling like vultures on them, to bear away the remnants, believing they worked wonders for all those who came and prayed or petitioned them. Men had grown mad with zeal at their belief in the unbelievable and their love for the unloveable. Yes, they built churches and basilicas to their new God and housed the remnants of their saints within as focal points for those needing to be cured of sin or maladies.

The ancient god sat brooding a while longer on the matter, thinking how his own temples reflected only beauty, grace and elegance, containing sculptured statues of himself, Athena, Hera, Demeter or other members of his family, and all were nobly executed. The images that men had formerly made of him had pleased him greatly. Yet Christians now created images of their holy saints with long, unnatural bodies; they gave them eyes like fish and each holy saint had the appearance of being strung up by the neck to heaven with a halo round his head. When art itself set the intellectual eye to see awry, what hope was there for him, Lord Zeus, to draw the human mind back from the unnatural when only the extraordinary seemed pleasing to it?

Lord Zeus groaned aloud and looked now at his family. With one accord they felt his eyes on them and stood stock-still expectantly. A movement from him and they would obey him instantly in anything that he desired.

"My family," Zeus said at last, "we must put an end to this absurdity in men! I see they have defiled our sanctuaries with Christian churches. Let us shake the earth to its foundations and rid our holy sites of them. What do you say, my brother?"

Poseidon, god of the sea and instigator of mighty earthquakes too, seized his trident (so similar in size and shape to the three-pronged peninsula of Chalkidiki). "At last you speak!" he cried. "At last you give instructions to destroy this Christian enemy!"

"Have we not already fought off this invasion?" went on almighty Zeus. "Did we not do our best to dispel Jehovah's claim on our own people? Did we not cause men to persecute the Christians, or did we not send the plague amongst them, only to find that those faithful to their Christian worship showed themselves more admirable than ever, the more suffering they endured? My brother! I no longer care for men as once I cared. They no longer care for me, or those who do care are forbidden to make sacrifice or worship me, so we have seceded from our past concern for them. Jehovah is inviolable! Nevertheless, some things hurt me beyond measure and I think it an impertinence that it has come about. I will not tolerate the churches on my sacred sites! Let us shake the earth, my brother, and destroy these new basilicas that have been built! Bring down the stones that have been erected to Jehovah!"

Poseidon's ravaged face was set as though an earth convulsion had already ravaged it. He said: "It is the very least that we should do! Let us tumble those edifices! Let us flood the rivers so that all that was once dear to us becomes a swamp! Let us obliterate the things we find abhorrent to us! The fear we put in men will surely turn them to us once again?"

"My brother," said Lord Zeus, "I do not hold out hope for men to worship us again. I do not hope for that. I only think that we can make uncomfortable the lives of mortal men who've turned now to Jehovah and his Son, Jesus Christ. Let them do whatever they believe they should under his guidance, even if it be absurd and seems to us sheer lunacy. Let Jehovah test them to the point of madness, but let us not endure the sight of those Christian churches on our sacred land."

Poseidon was already gone! And in the course of time a fearful quake shook Olympia the site of the Olympic Games, and the rivers (those living streams of life beside the holy site) clung in terror to each other and engulfed the sanctuary where Lord Zeus had his mighty temple and his wife, Hera, too, and where a basilica had been built where no Christian church should be. The columns of the temples fell, the walls of the church and all the statues and the stands and stadiums shattered or were submerged in water and the silt washed down in fear and terror by the living streams of rivers which stayed quivering and clinging to each other. The same happened at Dodona where Lord Zeus was affronted at the basilica built there and where his sacred oak tree had been savagely uprooted by those Christian people. So too did a great quake engulf the sacred site at nearby Dion where the basilica was shaken from its foundations and was left fragmented and in ruins. But Lord Poseidon spared the Parthenon at Athens. The holy edifice still pleased the gods. Let it house the Christian church! To destroy the mighty works of excellence would be more painful to the gods than to leave them as a reminder to the mortal mind of what had once been under their own guidance.

But other things perturbed Lord Zeus and again he voiced his thoughts aloud.

"I have been informed of something strange and worrying to my mind, my family," he began. "Listen now to what I have to say." There was a stirring of his family's limbs as they settled down to listen to the mighty words.

Zeus went on: "There are many who have stayed faithful to us but who can no longer make sacrifice to us without persecution or being put to death by the Christians who profess to love their neighbours as themselves. I fear, though, for those remaining followers of ours. I fear that soon they will be confounded by the Christian manner of drawing them too into their company by wily means. These humble followers of ours now hear our names repeated by the priests and bishops in the name of Christ. They hear Christians sending up petitions in our names but under the guise of their holy saints. A martyr by the name of Zeus even! Yes! A soldier who professed the Christian faith in Alexandria was martyred there and they say his name was Zeus! Zeus is dead! He died in the name of Christ! You too, my wife! Our poor followers no longer know what to believe. They now pray to these new holy figures who appear to them on icons bearing the names of many of us." And the eyes of Zeus found the eyes of Hermes, and the head of Zeus nodded. "Yes, you are one, my son! Agios Hermes – Holy Hermes or, as some say, Saint Hermes. There are too Agios Apollo, Agios Dionysios, Heraies, Demetrius – And, where we once watched over some area of their human lives, the Christians now have saints usurping our authority. They have used your name, my sister, but have changed your sex so now you are invoked by those who love you still but as Agios Demetrius. Thus it seems we cannot rise up from our vanquished state because the Christians have cast over us a net so finely spun and of such strength that we are bound within it, unable to escape but used within it for their Christian purpose of conversion and of victory.

"Why should we mind? I see that we are used by Christians for their explanations to those who doubt the truth of Christianity, that all that's gone before of beauty, good and right, was only beautiful and good and right because all along Jehovah was supreme and we were subservient. Is that not of all things unbelievable? But if men choose to have faith in the unfathomable, to believe the unbelievable and think natural the unnatural, then we can do no more to draw them back to us.

"My family! I have pondered long enough! Let us now throw off our garbs of mourning and let us instead rejoice! We are spared the trammels of our responsibilities to men! We need no longer pay heed to them in their distress and their petitioning. Instead, we can now watch their plans unfold beneath us as on a map spread out for all to see who have a wish to see. Let us instead rejoice that now we have no need to act! Come! Let us hear music once again! Let us recharge our goblets, fill them up with nectar! Let us once more fulfill those words of the great poet who spoke about the laughter of the gods. We are free, so let us laugh again!"

BIBLIOGRAPHY

Aeschylus: *Seven Plays in English Verse, translated by Lewis Campbell, M.A.* Oxford University Press, 1906.

Aristophanes: *Clouds, translated by Alan H. Sommerstein.* Penguin Books, 1973

Camp, John M: *The Athenian Agora, Excavations in the Heart of Classical Athens*, Thames and Hudson, 1992.

Cook, B.F: *The Elgin Marbles*, The Trustees of the British Museum, 1984.

Dawkins, Richard: *Science in the Soul*, Penguin Random House, 2017.

Dudley, Jill: *Ye Gods! (Travels in Greece)*, Orpington Publishers, 2006.

Dudley, Jill: *Ye Gods! II (More travels in Greece)*, Orpington Publishers, 2008.

Dudley, Jill: *Lap of the Gods (Travels in Crete and the Aegean islands)*, Orpington Publishers, 2015.

Dudley, Jill: *Gods & Heroes (On the trail of the Iliad and the Odyssey)*, Orpington Publishers, 2018.

Dudley, Jill: *Behind the Masks (In the footsteps of the early Greek dramatists)*, Orpington Publishers, 2020.

Euripides: *Plays of Euripides, translated by Shelley, R. Potter & M. Wodhull, Vol. I*, J.M. Dent & Sons Ltd., 1906.

Euripides: *Bacchae, Edited with Introduction and Commentary by E.R. Dodds*, Oxford University Press, 1960.

Freyne, Seán: *Galilee, from Alexander the Great to Hadrian, 323 BCE to 135 CE*, T & T Clark Ltd., 1980.

Grant, Michael & John Hazel: *Who's Who in Classical Mythology*, Weidenfeld & Nicolson, 1993.

Graves, Robert: *The Greek Myths: I & II*, Penguin Books Ltd., 1986.

Greece, the Blue Guide, A & C Black Publishers Ltd., 1990.

Greece, the Rough Guide, Penguin Books, 1995.

Grigson, Geoffrey: *The Goddess of Love*, Constable & Co. Ltd., 1976.

Herodotus: *The Histories of Herodotus, translated by Harry Carter*, Oxford University Press, 1962.

Harvey, Sir Paul: *The Oxford Companion to Classical Literature*, Oxford University Press, 1974.

Hesiod: *Theogony, translated by Richard Clay*, Penguin Books Ltd., 1985.

Homer: *The Iliad, translated by Martin Hammond*, Penguin Books Ltd., 1987.

Homer: *The Odyssey, translated by Richmond Lattimore*, Harper Perennial, 1967.

Hughes, Bettany: *The Hemlock Cup*, Vintage, 2011

Johnson, Paul: *Socrates, a Man for our Times*, Penguin Books, 2011.

Kagan, Donald: *Pericles of Athens and the Birth of Democracy*, The Free Press, A Division of Macmillan, Inc., 1991.

Kerényi, Carl: *Dionysos*, Princeton University Press, 1996.

Lang, Andrew: *The Homeric Hymns (a new prose translation)*, George Allen, London, 1899.

Papathanassopoulos, Dr. G: *The Acropolis, A New Guide of the Monuments and Museum*, 'Krene' edition, 1991.

Parke, H.W: *Greek Oracles*, Hutchinson & Co. (Publishers) Ltd., 1967.

Pausanias: *Guide to Greece, volumes 1 & 2*, Penguin Books Ltd. 1971.

Plato: *The Collected Dialogues of Plato, edited by Edith Hamilton and Huntington Cairns*, Princeton University Press, 1961.

Plato: *Defence of Socrates, Euthyphro, and Crito, translation by David Gallop*, Oxford University Press, 1997.

Plato: *Phaedo, translated by David Gallop*, Oxford University Press, 1997.

Plato: *Republic, translated by Robin Waterfield*, Oxford University Press, 1993.

Plato: *The Symposium, translated by Walter Hamilton*, Penguin Books Ltd., 1951.

Plutarch: *Greek Lives, translated by Robin Waterfield*, Oxford University Press, 1998.

Radice, Betty: *Who's Who in the Ancient World*, Penguin Books, 1973.

Scully, Vincent: *The Earth, the Temple, and the Gods*, Yale University Press, 1962.

Taylor, A.E: *Plato, The Man and His Work*, Dover Publications, Inc., New York, 2001.

Thucydides: *The Peloponnesian War, translated by Martin Hammond*, Oxford University Press, 2009.

Xenophon: *Conversations of Socrates, translated by Hugh Tredennick and Robin Waterfield*, Penguin Books, 1990.

GLOSSARY

ACHILLES
Greek hero of the Trojan War, son of King Peleus and Thetis, a minor sea-goddess.

ADMETUS
King of Pherae, husband of Alcestis.

AEGEUS
King of Athens and father of Theseus.

AEGISTHUS
Cousin of King Agamemnon and his brother Menelaus, later to become the lover of Clytemnestra.

AESCHYLUS
One of the three great Athenian dramatists c.525-456 B.C.

AGAMEMNON
King of Mycenae and brother of Menelaus. He was commander-in-chief of the Greek army in the Trojan War. On his return he was murdered by his wife Clytemnestra.

AGATHON
An Athenian tragic poet who won first prize at the Lenaia festival and celebrated it with a symposium as reported in Plato's dialogue *Symposium*.

AGORA
The civic centre of ancient Athens, where citizens met formally and informally to trade and to discuss important issues.

ALCESTIS
Wife of King Admetus. Famous for sacrificing her life so that her husband could live.

ALCIBIADES
c.450-404 B.C. Of noble birth, who had everything going for him but became dissolute. A would-be lover of Socrates.

ALEXANDER (the Great)
356-323 B.C. King of Macedonia, son of Philip II and Olympias.

AMALTHEA
The goat who suckled the infant Zeus.

AMPHITRITE
A Nereid, and wife of Poseidon.

ANYTUS
A wealthy Athenian tanner and industrialist. A democrat who was popular with the people. He was one of the three prosecutors of Socrates, and it was he who financed the trial.

APHRODITE
Goddess of love. Believed to be either the daughter of Zeus and Dione (an earth-goddess), or was born from the foam caused by the testicles of Ouranos when his son Kronos castrated him and flung them into the sea; she rose fully grown from the waves at Paphos, Cyprus. Her husband was Hephaestus.

APOLLO
Son of Zeus and Leto, and twin brother of Artemis. He was god of music, archery and prophecy.

APOLOGY
A dialogue by Plato about Socrates' defence at his trial.

ARCHELAUS
King of Macedonia from 413-399 B.C. He was keen to bring Athenian culture to his kingdom.

ARES
God of war. Lover of Aphrodite.

ARIADNE
Daughter of King Minos. She helped Theseus kill the Minotaur then ran away with him to Naxos.

ARISTOPHANES
Great Athenian comic dramatist c.448-c380 B.C.

ARTEMIS
Daughter of Zeus and Leto, and twin sister of Apollo. She was goddess of hunting and archery and, paradoxically, protector of wild life, young children and weak things.

ASCLEPIUS
God of medicine and healing, son of Apollo and the mortal woman Coronis.

ATHENA
Daughter of Zeus and Metis (his first wife) whom he swallowed because an oracle had warned she would next time bear a son who would overthrow his supremacy. Athena was goddess of wisdom, of weaving and all handicraft; she was also protectress of Athens.

BACCHANTES
(See Maenads.)

BOULEUTERION
Athens' council house in the Agora.

CADMUS
Founder of the city of Thebes, and great-great-grandfather of Oedipus.

CALCHAS
A seer and priest of Apollo who accompanied King Agamemnon to the Trojan War.

CALLIOPE
One of the nine Muses, daughter of Zeus and Mnemosyne.

CASTOR
(See Dioscuri.)

CEBES
A young Pythagorean philosopher present at Socrates' discussion on the soul in the final hours before his death.

CENTAURS
Mythical beasts with the body of a horse and the head of a man.

CENTAURUS
The son of Ixion. Ixion raped a cloud which he mistakenly took to be the goddess Hera with whom he was enamoured. The Centaurs were his offspring.

CERBERUS
A monstrous dog with three heads guarding the entry to Hades.

CHAEREPHON
A well respected admirer of Socrates. He is best remembered for asking the Delphic oracle if anyone was wiser than Socrates.

CHARICLES
A politician, notorious as one of the Thirty Tyrants.

CHARON
The ferryman who was believed to row the dead across the river Styx to Hades.

CHEIRON
A centaur. Unlike his fellow centaurs, he was wise and just, and knowledgeable in music and medicine.

CIRCE
Daughter of Helios (the Sun), sister of King Aeetes of Colchis and aunt of Medea. An enchantress who, in Homer's *Odyssey* detains Odysseus for a year.

CITY DIONYSIA
(See Great Dionysia.)

CLEMENT OF ALEXANDRIA
Christian theologian c.150-c.215 A.D.

CLEON
Athenian politician and general during the Peloponnesian War. Died 422 B.C.

CLYTEMNESTRA
Wife of King Agamemnon, and sister of Helen. She took Aegisthus for her lover, and murdered her husband on his return from the Trojan War.

CRITO
One of Socrates' closest friends, from the same deme, or village, of Alopeke.

CRITO
A dialogue by Plato about Socrates and his friend Crito who attempts to persuade Socrates to escape from gaol.

CURETES
Semi-divine beings to whom the infant Zeus was entrusted by his mother Rhea. Their duty was to clash their cymbals to drown his cries so his whereabouts would not be detected by his father Kronos.

CYCLOPES
One-eyed giants who made thunderbolts for Zeus. Polyphemus, son of Poseidon, was one of them.

DEMETER
Goddess of corn and agriculture, mother of Persephone. Her sacred rites were known as the Eleusian Mysteries.

DIONYSOS
Son of Zeus and the mortal woman Semele, daughter of King Cadmus of Thebes. He was god of wine and drama.

DIOSCURI
Castor and Polydeuces, the 'heavenly twins'. They were the sons of Zeus and Leda, and brothers of Helen and Clytemnestra.

ERECHTHEUM
A building on the north side of the Acropolis, named after Erechtheus, a legendary king of Athens.

ERINYES
Otherwise known as the Furies. Ancient chthonic goddesses who rose from their subterranean slumbers to torment anyone guilty of family bloodshed.

EROS
God of love, possibly the son of Aphrodite and Ares.

EURYDICE
Bride of Orpheus. She tragically died of a snake bite. Orpheus was allowed down to Hades to bring her back to the upper world, but forgot the one condition that he must not look back at her, and so she vanished for ever.

EURIPIDES
Great Athenian tragic dramatist. c.480-406 B.C.

FURIES
(See Erinyes.)

GAIA
Personification of the earth. She was born out of primeval Chaos and gave birth alone to Ouranos (heaven). From Gaia and Ouranos came Kronos and Rhea.

GIANTS
Monstrous beings with human bodies but with serpents' tails attached to their legs. They were the offspring of Gaia (earth) who became pregnant with them from the spots of blood that fell on her from her Titan son Kronos' castration of his father Ouranos. They had to be destroyed by Olympian gods if they were to rule the world.

GORGONS
Hideous female sisters with glaring eyes and snakes for hair. Their heads were displayed on shields to terrify the enemy.

GRACES
The personification of beauty and grace. Three in number.

GREAT DIONYSIA
An annual five-day drama festival in Athens held around the end of March and beginning of April.

HADES
Brother of Zeus. He was god of the underworld and his queen was Persephone.

HECTOR
The eldest son of King Priam of Troy and his wife Hecuba, and brother of Paris. He was killed by Achilles.

HECUBA
Wife of King Priam of Troy, and mother of Hector and Paris.

HELEN
Daughter of Leda and Zeus. She became the wife of Menelaus, and they had a daughter Hermione. She was seduced by Paris and ran away with him to Troy which triggered the Trojan War.

HELIOS
The Sun.

HEPHAESTUS
Lame son of Zeus and Hera. He was god of fire and a master craftsman in metal-work. His wife was Aphrodite.

HERA
Wife of Zeus, goddess of women and marriage. Her jealousy of Zeus' extra-marital affairs caused her much suffering.

HERACLES
Son of Zeus and the mortal beauty Alcmena, wife of Amphitryon. He had great strength and courage, and is best remembered for his twelve labours. He became known as Hercules under the Romans.

HERMAE
Square pillars on top of which was a head of the god Hermes, protector of travellers. These Hermae stood in the Agora, and at crossroads. As the god was also a god of fertility, many Hermae had on them erect phalluses.

HERMES
Son of Zeus and the mortal woman Maia. He often acted as his father's messenger, and conducted the souls of the dead down to Hades.

HESIOD
Greek poet c.700 B.C. Author of *Theogony*.

HESTIA
Daughter of Kronos and Rhea. She was goddess of the hearth.

HIPPOCRATES
460-c.375 B.C. Famous Greek physician from the Aegean island of Kos.

HOMER
Composer of the two epic poems the *Iliad* and the *Odyssey*. He was believed to have lived c.700 B.C.

IACCHOS
A little heard of deity identified with Dionysos in Demeter's Greater Mysteries.

ICONOSTASIS
The sanctuary screen in Orthodox churches covered in icons.

ICTINUS
Chief architect of the Parthenon. He worked under the supervision of the sculptor Phidias.

IPHIGENIA
Daughter of King Agamemnon and Clytemnestra. She became a human sacrifice at Aulis in Greece in order to appease the goddess Artemis who was preventing the Greek ships from setting sail for Troy.

IRIS
Goddess of the rainbow and messenger of the gods.

IXION
An unwelcome would-be lover of Hera, who was tricked by Zeus into raping a cloud, the result of which was the birth of Centaurus.

JASON
Son of Aeson, the rightful king of Iolchos whose throne was usurped by Pelias. The latter promised to give up the throne if Jason brought him back the Golden Fleece from Colchis.

JEHOVAH
Jewish name for God in the Old Testament.

KORE
(See Persephone.)

KRONOS
Son of Ouranos (heavens) and Gaea (Mother Earth). He was father of Zeus, Hestia, Demeter, Hera, Poseidon and Hades by Rhea, his wife and sister.

LAMPROCLES
The eldest son of Socrates and Xanthippe.

LAPITHS
A Greek nation inhabiting northern Thessaly. They were often at war with the uncivilized Centaurs.

LEDA
Wife of King Tyndareus of Sparta, and mother of Clytemnestra, the Dioscuri and Helen.

LENAIA
An Athenian festival of drama held in January. It was of less importance than the Great Dionysia.

LIBANIUS
314-393 A.D. A rhetorician who studied in Athens before opening a school of rhetoric in Constantinople.

LYCON
An Athenian citizen. Little is known about him except he was one of the three men who prosecuted Socrates.

MAENADS
Women followers of Dionysos who, under his power, were seized with unnatural strength and, in a state of ecstatic frenzy, ran into the mountains where they tore apart wild beasts and devoured them. They wore fawn skins and carried a thyrsus (a staff crowned with a pine-cone).

MAIA
A nymph and mother of Hermes by Zeus.

MEDUSA
(See Gorgons.)

MELETUS
A young poet and religious fanatic. He was one of the three men who brought a prosecution against Socrates for impiety.

MENELAUS
Son of King Atreus of Mycenae, and brother of Agamemnon. He became king of Sparta when he married Helen.

METIS
The first love of Zeus, and mother of the goddess Athena.

MINOS
King of Crete, father of Ariadne and Phaedra. His wife was Pasiphae.

MINOTAUR
Half-man, half-bull, the son of Pasiphae, wife of King Minos of Crete and a white bull of Poseidon with whom she became besotted. The Minotaur lived on human flesh till Theseus killed it.

MNEMOSYNE
A Titaness, and the personification of Memory. She was the mother of the nine Muses who were fathered by Zeus.

MUSES
Nine daughters of Zeus and Mnemosyne. Each Muse presided over one of the arts or sciences.

NEREIDS
Daughters of Nereus who were semi-divine. One of them was Thetis who became the mother of Achilles.

NEREUS
A kindly sea-deity and father of Thetis the mother of Achilles.

NIKE
Portrayed as a winged figure. She was the personification of Victory.

ODYSSEUS
Son of King Laertes of Ithaka. He was married to Penelope and they had one son Telemachus. Odysseus was one of the most courageous and daring of the Greek warriors. His journey home after the Trojan War took ten years due to the anger of Poseidon. He is the hero of Homer's *Odyssey*.

OEDIPUS
King of Thebes who unwittingly killed Laius, his father, and married his mother Jocasta.

OLYMPIAN GODS
Generally said to be: Zeus, Hera, Athena, Apollo, Artemis, Ares, Demeter, Hephaestus, Aphrodite, Dionysos or Hestia, Hermes and Ares.

OLYMPIAS
Mother of Alexander the Great. She came from Dodona and was a devotee of Dionysos.

ORESTES
Son of King Agamemnon and Clytemnestra. After the murder of his father by his mother, Orestes killed his mother to avenge the murder of his father by her.

ORPHEUS
Son of one of the Muses, thought to be Calliope, possibly by Apollo. His singing was so divine that mountains would bow down to hear, and fish would jump from the sea. He was a devotee of Dionysos, but died at the hands of the frenzied Maenads, and his head, still singing, ended up on the Aegean island of Lesbos.

OURANOS
The personification of the Heavens who mated with Gaia (Mother Earth); their son was Kronos (Time) and Rhea, parents of Zeus and several other Olympian gods.

PANATHENAIA
The annual Athenian festival held in honour of the goddess Athena.

PARIS
Son of King Priam of Troy and Hecuba. It was he who ran off with Helen and triggered the Trojan War.

PARTHENON
The temple of Athena that crowns the Acropolis in Athens.

PASIPHAE
Wife of King Minos of Crete and mother of the Minotaur.

PATROCLUS
Beloved childhood friend of Achilles whose death in the Trojan War left Achilles desolate but brought him back into the war.

PAUSANIAS
110-c.180 A.D. Greek travel-writer who recounted what he saw of the ancient sites of interest in Greece.

PELOPONNESIAN WAR
431-404 B.C. An on-off war between Athens and her allies, and Sparta and her allies which lasted nearly thirty years.

PENELOPE
Wife of Odysseus.

PERICLES
A great Athenian statesman c.500-429 B.C.

PERSEPHONE
Daughter of the goddess Demeter, also known as Kore.

PHAEDO
A disciple of Socrates who was present at his death.

PHAEDO
A dialogue by Plato giving Phaedo's first-hand account of the last hours and death of Socrates.

PHIDIAS
c.475-c.425 B.C. A great Athenian sculptor responsible for the Parthenon marbles.

PLATO
c.428-347 B.C. Athenian philosopher and pupil of Socrates.

PLUTO
Name for Hades, meaning 'rich one'.

POLYDEUCES
(See Dioscuri.)

POLYPHEMUS
A one-eyed Cyclops and son of Poseidon.

POSEIDON
Brother of Zeus. He was god of the sea as well as of earthquakes and horses.

PRIAM
King of Troy, father of Hector and Paris. Married to Hecuba.

PROPYLAEA
The great entranceway to the Acropolis.

PYLADES
A lifelong friend and companion of Orestes.

PYTHIA
Apollo's priestess at Delph through whom he gave his prophetic pronouncements.

RHEA
Mother of Zeus and five other Olympian gods. (See Kronos.)

SATYRS
Followers of Dionysos. Lustful creatures half-human with the tails of a horse, and legs of a goat. They are equated with fertility.

SELENE
Identified with the moon in Greek antiquity before she was eclipsed by Artemis.

SEMELE
Daughter of King Cadmus of Thebes who was loved by Zeus. Hera, Zeus' jealous wife, persuaded her to ask Zeus to reveal himself to her in his full immortal glory, whereupon the young beauty was reduced to a cinder. The embryo of Dioysos was sewn into Zeus' thigh till he was ready to be born.

SILENUS
A Satyr noted for his wisdom. He became tutor to the young Dionysos.

SIMMIAS
A young Pythagorean philosopher who was present at Socrates' discussion on the Soul in his final hours before his death.

SOCRATES
Major Athenian philosopher 469-399 B.C.

SOPHISTS
Men of learning who demanded payment for giving lessons in mathematics, rhetoric and politics. They were expert quibblers.

SOPHOCLES
One of the three major Athenian tragic dramatists 496-406 B.C.

STYX
The river across which the dead were ferried to Hades.

SYMPOSIUM
A men-only drinking party. There was often entertainment such as flute-girls, dancers or acrobats.

SYMPOSIUM
A dialogue by Plato in which the main topic of conversation was Love.

TARTARUS
The underworld where the souls of sinners went after judgement.

THESEUS
National hero and king of Athens. He was the son of King Aegeus and Aethra, daughter of King Pittheus of Troezen, though it was also rumoured that the god Poseidon was his father.

THEAETETUS
A young man of budding intellect with whom Socrates discussed the subject of Knowledge as reported in Plato's dialogue *Theaetetus*.

TITANS AND TITANESSES
Offspring of Ouranos and Gaea, often confused with the Giants. Both came into conflict with the Olympian gods.

TYNDAREUS
King of Sparta, father of Helen, Clytemnestra and the Dioscuri by his wife Leda, though Zeus was also said to be the father of Helen.

XANTHIPPE
Wife of Socrates.

XENOPHON
An ardent admirer of Socrates, and author of *Memoirs* – biographical jottings of his meetings with Socrates.

ZEUS

Supreme god of the Olympians. He was married to Hera but had many extra-marital affairs with mortal and immortal beauties, by whom he fathered many gods and demi-gods.

INDEX

Achilles 14, 115
Acropolis 1, 3, 5, 17, 28, 33, 34-6, 68, 86
Acts of the Apostles 87
Admetus, King 39
Adonis 43, 44
Aegean 73, 80, 90, 108, 109, 110, 112
Aegina, island 90, 129
Aegeus, King 62, 68
Aegisthus 27
Aeschylus 22, 27, 71
Aesop 105
Agamemnon, King 27, 68, 70, 115
Agathon 39, 41
Agora 5, 6, 7, 12, 13, 51, 52, 84, 87
Alcestis 39
Alcibiades 22, 37ff, 54, 97
Alexander, the Great 111
Allah 123
Alopeke 2, 80
Altar of the Twelve Gods 5, 13, 52
Amphitrite 90, 99
Ancient Antissa 109
Aphrodite 37ff
Aphrodite's Grotto 43, 44, 46
Apollo 59, 61-71, 75, 105, 107, 122, 124,
Apology 61 33, 51ff
Archelaus, King 5, 6, 10, 30
Areópagus 28, 86
Ares 42
Ariadne 62
Aristophanes 22, 31-33, 39-41
Artemis 59, 63, 69ff

Artemis Brauronia 72
Asclepiad 123
Asclepeion 123
Asclepius 120ff
Athena 8, 12, 28, 29, 33, 57, 71, 86, 89, 90, 123
Athens 1, 2, 3, 5, 12, 16, 19, 23, 26, 28, 51, 54, 57, 58, 62, 63, 6497, 99, 129
Athos, Mt. 95, 96
Atlantis 92ff

Bacchae 31
Bacchus 111
Bacchantes (see Maenads)
Battle of the Gods and Giants 11, 13, 90
Battle of the Lapiths and Centaurs 87, 90
Bears, Little 72
Belief 88, 112, 131
Beauty 58
Bolshoi Ballet 33ff
Bouleuterion 58
Brauron 71, 72

Cadmus, King 29, 30
Calliope 107
Castalian, spring 67
Cebes 111
Centaurs 90
Centaurus and Lapiths, Battle of 90
Cerberus 11, 87
Chaerephon 54, 98
Chalkidiki 97

Charicles 51, 52
Charmides 98
Chaos 42
Charon 22, 107
Cheiron 14, 15
Christ 16, 23, 88, 107, 111, 123
Christian, Christianity 2, 12, 19, 23, 27, 31, 48, 69, 76, 110, 111, 123
Christodoulos, Osios 75
City Dionysia 26
Clement of Alexandria 23
Clouds 32, 33
Clytemnestra 27
Constantine, St. 56
Corinth 99, 100
Corinthians 97
Courage 7
Crane Dance 62, 63
Crete 9, 61, 66, 175ff, 92
Critas 51, 98
Crito 71-68, 118, 120, 127ff
Crito 79-88
Cyclades, islands 62
Cyclops 91
Cynthos, Mt. 64
Cyprus 42ff, 100

Darwin 125
Dawkins, Richard 125
Death 81, 105ff, 112ff
Delian Games 62, 63
Delian League 3, 65, 97
Delos 59, 61ff, 106
Delphi 66ff, 111, 124
Delphic, oracle 27, 28, 54
Demeter 19-23, 50, 107, 111
Democracy 86
Diktaon cave 9-10
Dikte, Mt. 9
Diometa 41

Dion 108
Dionysos 26, 62, 107, 108, 110
Dionysos Eleuthereus 26, 29
Dioscuri (see Castor and Polydeuces)
Dodona 159, 160
Duty 49

Easter 19, 24ff
Eileithyia 64
Eleusian Mysteries 21, 22, 50, 107
Eleusis 20, 111
Eleusian sanctuary 20-22
Elysium 22
Ephesus 72, 73, 100
Epidaurus 121, 129
Erinyes (see Furies)
Eros 41, 42
Euboea 90
Eumenides 29
Euripides 30, 31, 70
Eurydice 107, 108

Faith 88, 113
Fira 93ff
Furies 2, 8, 29, 68, 72

Gaia 8, 42, 66
Gentile 111
Gods and Giants, battle of 90
God 3, 6, 7, 31, 52, 53, 74-78, 88, 106, 114, 123, 125ff
Gortyn, Crete 75ff
Great Dionysia, festival 26ff
Greek Orthodox Church 23-26, 75, 126

Hades 20ff, 39, 107, 111, 115
Helena, St. 56
Helios 42
Hellenize 111
Hephaestus 8, 42, 86, 87

Hephaisteion 87
Hera 14, 29, 42, 63, 64
Heracles 81
Hermes 50
Hermae 49, 110
Herodes Atticus, theatre 33
Hesiod 11, 42
Hestia 55, 56
Hill of the Muses 86
Hippocrates 113, 124
Hippocratic Oath 123
Hippolytus 122
Holy Mountain, see Athos, Mt.
Homer 6, 13, 64, 66, 70, 91ff
Hygiea 123
Hymettos Mts. 90

Iconostasis 24, 25
Iliad 6, 101
Inner Voice 3, 4, 79
Iphigenia 70ff
Iphigenia at Aulis 70
Iphigenia in Taurus 71
Island of the Blessed 22
Isthmian Games 99
Ixion 14

Jason 14ff
Jesus (see Christ)
Jews 111
John, the Theologian 73ff
Julian the Apostate 68

Kallichoron well 21, 22
Kassandra 97
Kenchreai 100
Kenchrias 100
Knowledge 7, 88, 98, 113, 131
Kollones Agoraios, hill 86
Kore (see Persephone)

Kos 122ff
Kronos 8, 9, 42

Labyrinth 61, 62
Lamprocles 104, 118
Lapiths 15, 87, 90
Law, Athenian 81ff
Lechaion 100
Lechis 100
Lenaia 26, 31, 39, 41
Lesbos 108
Leto 63, 64, 70
Lithos 52
Litochoro 52
Love 38ff

Macedonia 31
Maenads 26, 108
Maia 58
Medusa 63
Meletus 52
Memoirs, of Xenophon 38
Mercury 110
Metis 8
Michael, St 74
Michael, the Archangel 110
Minoan 72
Minos, King 61, 62
Minotaur 61, 62
Mnemosyne 101
Muses 122
Mycenae 71, 121
Mysteries, Demeter's Greater 19-22
Mysteries, Demeter's Lesser 19

Nauflio 121
Naxos 62
Nereid 100
Nereus 90
Nike 13, 57

Oath Stone 52
Odysseus 91ff, 115
Odyssey 6, 91ff, 115
Oedipus, King 68
Olympia 56ff
Olympian gods 3, 8, 14, 42
Olympias 56, 57
Olympic Games 55ff, 99
Olympus, Mt. 10, 11, 56, 64, 95, 108
Oressteia 27, 71
Orestes 27, 28, 68, 71, 86
Orpheus 39, 107ff, 111
Orphism 107, 111
Orthodox Church (see Greek Orthodox Church)
Ouranos 8, 42

Palestine 111
Panacea 123
Panagia Evangelistria 126
Panathenaia 12, 13, 123
Panathenaic Way 12, 13, 26
Paphos, Cyprus 42
Parnassus, Mt. 67
Parthenon 1, 3, 5, 8, 12, 13, 16, 17, 34, 87, 89
Pasiphae 61
Patmos 73ff
Paul, St. 72, 76, 87, 88, 99, 100, 101,
Pausanias 39, 99
Peirene 100
Pelion, Mt. 14
Peloponnese 1, 20, 56, 99, 121
Peloponnesian War 50, 51
Pentelicon Mt. 5
Pericles 2, 3, 8, 17, 22, 86, 87, 128
Persephone 20, 21, 23, 107, 111
Persians 13, 14, 50, 68
Peter, St. 22
Phaedo 114, 115, 120
Phaedo 103ff

Phaedrus 39
Phidias 13
Philosophy 7
Piety 88
Piraeus 80, 101
Plato 7, 8, 33, 37ff, 51ff, 92, 97ff, 103ff, 113
Pluto 115
Polydeuces (see Dioscuri)
Polyphemus 91ff
Poseidon 61, 63, 89, 90-101
Potidaea 97
Prison, of Socrates 81
Prytaneum 55, 56
Pylades 71
Pythia 67, 68
Python 67

Resurrection 23, 87, 88, 113
Rhea 9
Roman Catholic 113
Royal Stoa 5

Sacred Way 20, 67
Salamis 19, 30
Santorini 92ff
Saronic gulf 19, 80, 90, 1oo
Satyrs 26
Semele 29
Shelter of the Queen 44
Silas 87
Simmias 111, 113
Socrates 2, 3, 5, 6, 12, 13, 15, 19, 22, 27, 29-33, 37, 38, 44, 47ff, 51ff, 66, 72, 78, 79-88, 91, 103ff
Sophist 33
Sophocles 22
Soul 54, 106ff, 112ff
Sounion 80, 89, 90
Sparta 50
Stoa Basileios 5, 6, 12, 52

Styx, river 2, 63
Sun 21
Symposium 37
Symposium 7, 37ff, 54, 97, 108

Tartarus 22, 42
Taurus 71
Taxiarchis, monastery 110
Telesterion 21, 22
Thebes 29, 30
Theseus 62, 87, 122
Thessaly 15
Thirty Tyrants 51
Timothy 87
Tinos, island 126
Titan/Titaness 8, 63
Titus, St. 76
Trojans 6

Trojan War 14, 27, 70, 101
Truth 58

Virgin Mary 96, 126ff, 130
Virtue 7

Wisdom 54
Women 69

Xanthippe 2, 7, 103
Xenophon 5, 38, 39, 51, 104

Zeus 8, 10-12, 14, 21, 29, 32, 42, 50, 56, 57, 58, 63, 67, 86, 95, 122

ALSO BY JILL DUDLEY:

Ye Gods!
(Travels in Greece)

Ye Gods! II
(More travels in Greece)

Holy Smoke!
(Travels in Turkey and Egypt)

Gods in Britain
(An island odyssey from pagan to Christian)

Mortals and Immortals
(A satirical fantasy & true-in-parts memoir)

Holy Fire!
(Travels in the Holy Land)

Lap of the Gods
(Travels in Crete and the Aegean Islands)

Gods & Heroes
(On the trail of the Iliad & the Odyssey)

Behind the Masks
(In the footsteps of the early Greek dramatists)

'Put it in Your Pocket' booklets

BIOGRAPHY

Jill Dudley was born in Baghdad and educated in England. Her first play was performed by the Leatherhead Repertory Company, since when she has written plays and short stories for radio. She returned to Iraq briefly while her husband was working out there and, when they came back to England, they bought a dairy farm. They retired from farming in 1990 since when she has travelled extensively around Greece, Turkey and Egypt and a number of her travel articles have appeared in the national newspapers followed in quick succession by her popular travel-writing books.

Website: www.orpingtonpublishers.co.uk